. . . there are quite a number of areas . . . where the probability is quite high that large unidentified animals still exist waiting for our curious eyes.

Dr. Roy P. Mackal
Associate in Biology
Office of the President
University of Chicago
Department of Biology

. . . Every year, an average of three or four amphibians, two or three reptiles, as many birds, and nearly a dozen mammals are discovered.

Dr. Bernard Heuvelmans
Centre de Cryptozoologie,
France

CHAMP –
Beyond the Legend
(Updated Edition)

By JOSEPH W. ZARZYNSKI

Joseph W. Zarzynski

M-Z INFORMATION

By JOSEPH W. ZARZYNSKI
CHAMP — BEYOND THE LEGEND
(Updated Edition)

1st Edition 1984, Bannister Publications

2nd Edition 1988, M–Z Information

Copyright 1988 Joseph W. Zarzynski

Published by M–Z Information
P.O. Box 2129
Wilton, New York 12866 USA

Library of Congress Catalog Card Number 88–060702

ISBN 0–937559–01–6

Printed in the United States of America by
Capital City Press, Inc., Montpelier, Vermont

Cover designed by Capital City Press, Inc. Photo cover is of the 1977 Mansi photograph
purported to be of the "Lake Champlain Monster."
Photo copyright/credit: Sandra Mansi/Gamma Liaison.

To my Mother and Father—who have instilled in me a passion for wildlife, history, exploring, and mysteries.

To Pat—a much cherished prize and my associate during cryptozoological expeditions.

To my friends and cryptozoologists—for the camaraderie we have shared.

To Champ—for providing me with a formidable "legend" to pursue.

Above:
The Lake Champlain Sea Serpent — a woodcut by T. Tobin of the Swanton, Vermont Courier newspaper — circa 1880. *(courtesy: O'Shea Publishing)*

Left:
Reports of monstrous aquatic creatures have long intrigued us as in this 1567 visual of the "Great Norwegian Sea Serpent," from Olaus Magnus Historia de Gentibus Septentrionalibus. *(courtesy: Fortean Picture Library)*

THE Lake Champlain phenomena (less objectively, unidentified animals) are extremely important for the question of the so-called "Lake Monsters." Although there is a great deal of evidence for "Lake Monsters" in lakes and rivers between 40° and 60° N. Latitude, other than Loch Ness, the best photographic evidence comes from Lake Champlain. The importance of this evidence rests in the fact that it establishes that while these relatively rare creatures are extremely elusive and surreptitious in behavior, they are nevertheless ubiquitous in distribution.

These phenomena are not unique parochial anomalies confined to a single lake such as Loch Ness. This is an important conclusion — since it negates the idea that a special set of natural conditions or human activities, such as frauds and hoaxes, are responsible for the reported observations.

Getting back to the Lake Champlain evidence, possibly the best still photograph ever obtained of these creatures is the Sandra Mansi photograph. From a zoological point of view, this photograph passes muster as a genuine shot of an unidentified animal. All subsequent analysis of this picture have tended to confirm this interpretation.

Photographs or films, no matter how good, will never settle the matter. A specimen, preferably a live one, will be required for that. Then and only then will we be able to arrive at a final classification of these creatures.

DR. ROY P. MACKAL
Associate in Biology
Office of the President
University of Chicago
Department of Biology

Table of Contents

Illustrations

Acknowledgements

THIS BOOK is the result of my 14 years of research and field work into the Champ phenomenon. Much of the impetus for CHAMP— BEYOND THE LEGEND goes to Bob DuBois, who commissioned me to write an article on Champ in 1982 for Bannister Publications' initial issue of *Adirondack Bits 'n Pieces* magazine. That article was so well received that it induced Bob to ask me to follow it up with a Champ booklet. However, eventually the monstrous form of the Champ animals carried over into its literary counterpart and the booklet undertook a metamorphosis in 1984 into the first nonfiction Champ book.

I do hope that CHAMP—BEYOND THE LEGEND will etch on record the Champ saga as I know it and will chronicle the activities of the search efforts.

The research and the writing of this book involves an indebtedness and appreciation to so many individuals and organizations. This list appears almost endless, but it is certainly necessary.

First, I would like to express my gratitude and love to my parents, Grandmother, and relatives for the years of encouragement. And to those special friends who probably without knowing have been my pillars of vigor and refreshment throughout all these Champ and Nessie campaigns and even the years before: Margaret & Charlie Kuenzel, Jim & Carol Randesi, David Williams, Bruce Bookhout, David Dibler, Ken Nigh, John

Bierman, Betsy & David Gibbs, David Pitkin, "Waples Raiders," Thomas Wheatley, Jim Burke, Don Gevert and many other valued companions.

I would also like to praise those cryptozoologists and scientists of other disciplines whose labors at Loch Ness, Scotland have directly aided me in beginning to unlock the portal at Lake Champlain: Tim Dinsdale, Dr. Robert Rines, Ivor Newby, David James, Marty Klein, Nicholas Witchell, Lionel Leslie, "Doc" Edgerton, Adrian Shine, Dick Raynor, Alex Campbell, Dr. Roy P. Mackal, Bob Rickard, J. Richard Greenwell, Rip Hepple, F.W. Holiday, Dr. Henry H. Bauer, Jim Hogan, Tony Healy, Father Gregory Brusey, Robin Holmes, Tony Harmsworth, Dr. George Zug, Dr. Bernard Heuvelmans, and others.

My files overflow with research material on Champ, crypto-zoology, and Forteana in great part due to the exchange of information with: Larry Arnold, George W. Earley, Lucius Farish, Gary S. Mangiacopra, Janet & Colin Bord, Warren Thompson, Robert Jones, Dwight Whalen, Mayor Erastus Corning II, Tim Church, Mike Frizzell, Ray W. Boeche, Richard Smith, Bruce G. Hallenbeck, Jean-Pierre Sylvestre, Dr. Forrest Wood, Peter Byrne, Dave Waters, Bob & Paul Bartholomew, David Salonin, Clive Cussler, Ted Straiton, John Becker, Loren Coleman, and a host of other dedicated and unselfish researchers.

The Champ story has unfolded before us partly because of the curiosity and journalistic skills of these members of the media: Richard Cowperthwait, David Herd, Ron Kermani, Lois Clermont, Jeff Wright, Barney Fowler, Fred Wilson, Elizabeth Owen, Don Tinney, Merritt Clifton, George Fowler, Mike Connery, John Noble Wilford, Bob Studley, Alan Darling, Pete Horton, Francee Covington, Steve LaRose, Bob Curtis, Sherrill L. McGill, Hal Smith, Ellsworth Boyd, Pamela Weintraub, Carol Hemingway, Shaun Levesque, Brian Vachon, Rod Canham and these newspapers, periodicals, and magazines: *Burlington Free Press, Plattsburgh Press Republican, Binghamton Press, Binghamton Sun-Bulletin, Albany Times-Union, Schenectady Gazette, The Saratogian, Times of Ti, The Islander, Christian Science Monitor, The North*

Countryman, Rutland Herald, OMNI, Life, Glens Falls Post Star, The ISC Newsletter, Pursuit, INFO Journal, Fortean Times, Ness Information Service Newsletter, Metroland, Whitehall Times, Addison County Independent, and the dozens of radio and television stations that have been of immense assistance to me over the past few years.

Many societies, organizations, associations, and groups, too, have been highly supportive and have given assistance to my research and cryptozoological field projects. Some of these are: Feinberg Library — SUNY/Plattsburgh, Vermont Historical Society, Vermont State Library, International Society of Cryptozoology, SITU, INFO, Lake Champlain Committee, Champlain Maritime Society, New York State DEC, Vermont Division for Historic Preservation, Vermont Agency for Environmental Conservation, Saratoga YMCA Scuba Club, New York State Diver's Association, Ithaca College, Aqualung Diving Center, Vestigia, and Saratoga Nautilus.

Two notable organizations affiliated with the well-being of Lake Champlain are the Lake Champlain Committee and the Champlain Maritime Society. The Lake Champlain Committee is an environmental group concerned with the safeguard of the lake's ecology. The Champlain Maritime Society is "dedicated to the identification and preservation of maritime knowledge, artifacts and underwater or land-based sites pertinent to the history of the Lake Champlain Basin." For information contact:

LAKE CHAMPLAIN COMMITTEE   CHAMPLAIN MARITIME SOCIETY
14 SOUTH WILLIAMS STREET   P.O. BOX 745
BURLINGTON, VERMONT   BURLINGTON, VERMONT
05401 USA   05402 USA

Acknowledgements must, too, be directed to these people for their contributions to the "Champ cause": Anthony Mansi, Sandra Mansi, Alan Neigher, Dean Coon, Robert Hohmann, Tim Titus, Greg Furness, John Ray, Tony Ryan, Lauren Brownell, Donald Fangboner, Dr. Kempton Webb, Robert Brown, Frank Pollock, Richard Dickinson, Robert W. Carroll, Jr., Dr. William

H. Eddy, Jr., Charles Johnson, Millie Small, L. Nevil Davy, Doris Morton, Dr. Philip Reines, Connie Pope, Dr. George LaBar, Morris F. Glenn, Karen Ramsey, Marjorie Walter, Robert H. Politz, Spencer Tulis, Dick Hedges, Mr. & Mrs. Walter Washburn, Mr. & Mrs. Knight Washburn & Family, Lise Winer, Michael Bradley, Bob Cahill, Joan & Bob Blye, Richard Beckwith, Sue Hill, Marilyn Kennard and Father, Mike Veitch, Mike Valentine, "Noon" & John Meaney, Betty Harrington, Elaine Walcott, Nancy Miller, Helen Johnson, Judy & Paul Madison, John Foley, Bill Armstrong, Dewi Bowen, Jim Penny, Ray Manley, Tearlach MacFarlane, Jack Hughes, Chris & Gary Heurich, and the many others I have not the space to mention or may have forgotten.

I am extremely grateful for the illustrative visuals already acknowledged in the text and to those contributors who have, too, helped to inspire me in my cryptozoological endeavors. I would like to also acknowledge the efforts of these highly professional individuals for helping to make the appendices section of the book a solid reference "manual": Anne Platt, Monty Fischer, Fred Wilson, Dr. B. Roy Frieden, Dr. Paul H. LeBlond, Dr. Roy P. Mackal, J. Richard Greenwell, Dr. C.L. Smith, Dr. George Zug, and these honored bodies: the Port Henry, New York Village Board of Trustees, Vermont House of Representatives, New York State Senate, New York State Assembly, and the Vermont Senate.

Likewise, Bob DuBois and his lovely wife, Karen, deserve special applause and salutes for overseeing the birth of this Bannisterian project, the first nonfiction Champ book, originally published in 1984.

Sincere acknowledgements go to my elusive obsession, Champ, with a most sincere thanks!

And to M-Z Information for making this updated edition of CHAMP—BEYOND THE LEGEND a reality.

Finally, to Pat Meaney, my wife, for all her help in this glorious scientific quest.

Joseph W. Zarzynski

Foreword

The Search for *Champ, Nessie, Morag, Sea Serpents*, and other aquatic *monsters* and *unknowns* goes on from year to year with gathering momentum. With the recent formation of a bona fide scientific clearing house, and centre for the search, and research operations at Tucson, Arizona — we have in the International Society of Cryptozoology a most valuable forum — populated by specialists and true experts in many different fields, whose terms of reference enable them to bring initiative, open mindedness and enthusiasm to the difficult tasks that face the expeditioner, the technologist, and the fieldworker, who together make up an international team of no small proportion or ability.

Joseph W. Zarzynski — *Zarr* to his many friends and acquaintances, is one of these specialists, who has done more to quantify and qualify the fascinating sighting reports from Lake Champlain in recent times, than any other person. *CHAMP* — the lake's monstrous unknown animal — which seems to bear a striking resemblance to that reported from Loch Ness in Scotland, owes much to Zarr for his dogged perseverance, his determination to get to grips with the problem, and his balanced assessment of the data already recorded.

If, in the due course of time *CHAMP* is to be brought within the category of scientific zoology — from out of its present niche in the mysterious, and somewhat exciting obscurity of cryptozoology — much of the credit will be due to him.

TIM DINSDALE
Dec. 14, 1983 — Great Britain
The Loch Ness Association of Explorers

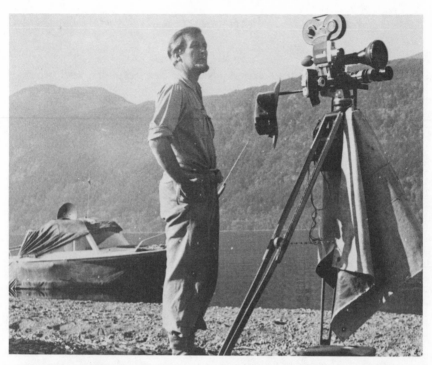

"Mr. Loch Ness," Tim Dinsdale, conducting a camera watch for Nessie at Foyers in 1972 with the support boat HUNTER in the background. Dinsdale has led the modern day scientific drive to solve the mystery of Loch Ness. He is the author of several books on Nessie and his field work at Loch Ness dates back to 1960. He is a member of the Royal Geographical Society and Explorers Club. Dinsdale and Zarzynski have long exchanged information on their respective searches at Loch Ness and Lake Champlain. In 1979 Dinsdale made Zarzynski an honorary member of his Loch Ness Association of Explorers. (© Tim Dinsdale, courtesy: Tim Dinsdale)

Publisher's Foreword

It is with great pleasure that M–Z Information brings you this updated edition of CHAMP – BEYOND THE LEGEND, the classic book on the Lake Champlain monsters, first published by Bannister Publications in 1984. M–Z Information acquired the publishing rights to CHAMP – BEYOND THE LEGEND in November, 1987. At that time the book was nearly out of print and there was an urgent demand to bring the book not only back into print, but to inform readers of new developments in the search for Champ.

This new edition will update the Champ story from 1984 to 1987. The book will also document more Champ sightings and shall describe the latest in technological gear deployed in looking for Champ. CHAMP – BEYOND THE LEGEND will also introduce you to some of the new people now involved in helping to solve the zoological mystery of Lake Champlain. But unfortunately, the book will also say good-bye to people who have passed away before all questions about Champ have been answered. These people – some pioneers of aquatic cryptozoology – have however left a legacy of research and faith in the quest that will allow others to push on for the eventual identification of the Champ animals. Since the publication of the first edition of CHAMP – BEYOND THE LEGEND in 1984, four noteworthy people mentioned in the text of this book have died. Three of them, Lionel Leslie, David James, and Tim Dinsdale, were very instrumental in the Loch Ness Investigation, an organization which led the way in investigating Nessie in the 1960s. Tony Mansi etched his name into the Champ chronicles with the now famous 1977 Mansi photograph of Champ, discussed by Joseph W. Zarzynski in this book. Through their tireless contributions the science of cryptozoology has crept closer to the final solution of what these puzzling aquatic animals are.

Minor changes and updates have been made in this new edition and a whole new section — Appendix 6 — has been added to make current the incredible Champ story. In doing so, Joseph W. Zarzynski and M–Z Information would like to thank the following individuals, organizations, and firms for their help in the search for Champ: Vince Capone, Chip D'Angelo, Garry Kozak, Dr. Russell Bellico, Don Mayland, Ralph Veve, Dan Couture, R. Duncan Mathewson III, Charlie McKinney, Pam Warner, Connie Foley, Al Blanche, Jim Schneider, Jacques Boisvert, Dr. Eugene Lepeschkin, Lori Fisher, Grace Pugh, Nina & Jason Bacon, the Atlantic Alliance Lake George Bateaux Research Team, the Atlantic Alliance for Maritime Heritage Conservation, Divers World, and Capital City Press.

The goals of M–Z Information in publishing this second edition of CHAMP — BEYOND THE LEGEND are to educate, to inform, and to make more people aware of the possibility that something rather large and unidentified swims in the depths of Lake Champlain.

Possibly one day someone will get that definitive photograph or other proof which will finally let us know what Champ is. It would be no surprise to discover that beside that camera carrying individual was a copy of CHAMP — BEYOND THE LEGEND!

—M. Patram Meaney

Preface

As a legend it dates back to the early 1600s. Its popularity first thrived in the late 1800s when Americana christened it the "Lake Champlain Sea Serpent." The saga matured until the 1970s when it finally achieved a status nearly akin to its Highland cousin, Nessie, Scotland's Loch Ness Monster. It now has several regionally recognizable nicknames – Champy; the Lake Champlain Monster; the Champ phenomenon; and, most frequently, Champ.

From the earliest reported sightings to the present, Champ has maintained an elusive nature, avoiding all but the unprepared observer. Today it remains a scientific enigma – an unidentified animal of large dimensions and possible prehistoric origins inhabiting an historic North American waterway; truly a cryptozoological jigsaw puzzle.

Even though the final picture is far from complete, we do have many pieces of the puzzle with which to work – numerous eyewitness sightings recorded in word and art form, a few intriguing photographs, one video segment, and tantalizing sonar readings. Far from definitive, these clues nevertheless indicate the possibility of a zoological and historical wealth so precious that Champ has been granted legislative protection. Yet its complete story, that of "North America's Loch Ness," awaits final documentation. The Lake Champlain mystery animal is an incredible zoological secret that is more than a myth, it is CHAMP – BEYOND THE LEGEND.

CHAPTER 1

Lake Champlain And Its Mystery Animal

THE deeply suntanned veteran fisherman quieted the trolling motor on his small aluminum runabout boat just a few yards offshore from me. I was busy packaging our sonar, scuba and boat equipment, having concluded another week's field work at Lake Champlain in search of Champ. It was August 26, 1983, hazy and breezy, with a threat of impending rain.

"They tell me you're looking for the Monster," said the solitary fisherman. I nodded and turned my attention to his conversation. We had seen one another nearly everyday that week, he passing by fishing and I conducting surface camera surveillance and sonar monitoring.

"You know, I never believed all that stuff about some Monster in this lake. I've been fishing these waters for two weeks a year for the past 20 years. I never believed it—until yesterday," commented the angler as he reeled in his line to check his lure.

"About 6:15 last night, a ways north of here, I saw it," he continued. "Damn strange, too. A huge water disturbance, then three waves or large humps appeared—black in color." He pointed northwest toward Big Snake Bay (known also as Snake Den Harbor) on the New York State side of Lake Champlain.

"I've seen just about everything on and in this lake—fish, logs, birds, scuba divers, boats. And whatever that was it certainly wasn't one of them or a boat wake. Champ, huh, I never thought I'd see it. I'm not saying publicly that's what I actually saw, but

I'm sure not saying it isn't either. The fish weren't biting last night. Maybe that'll help your research, huh? Keep looking. Believe me, I know something's there. Sure would like to know what it is!"

He gunned his boat's motor and was off, hoping to land another pike or bass before his vacation closed. I continued to sort and pack our gear wondering if our next expedition might produce the definitive evidence to prove Champ's existence. I, too, craved to find out what this glorious and secret animal is.

Champ – Myth Or Fact?

A few years back Champ, the unidentified mystery animal of Lake Champlain, was overwhelmingly believed to be a myth, a chimera, the product of zealous and overly imaginative minds. Today many of those same non-believers are more open-minded as the evidence for Champ's existence mounts. Champ research and scientific investigation, too, has legitimized itself and found its proper niche in cryptozoological research (the science of studying hidden animals).

Champ is said to be quite similar in appearance to Scotland's Nessie. Dark in color, serpentine, about 20 feet long or more, with a snake-like head, shy and very elusive. Over two hundred sightings of these creatures have been documented, along with other supportive evidence such as Indian folklore, several photographs, sonar targets, and other references.   .

It now seems scientifically feasible that Lake Champlain is the habitat of a mammoth-sized animal, probably a breeding colony of an unknown species or one thought to be long extinct.

Lake Champlain – The Setting

Vᴇʀᴍᴏɴᴛ historian Ralph Nading Hill, in his book, *Lake Champlain: Key to Liberty*, calls Lake Champlain "the most historic body of water in the western hemisphere: a silver dagger from Canada to the heartland of the American colonies that forged the destiny of France and England in America, and the United States."

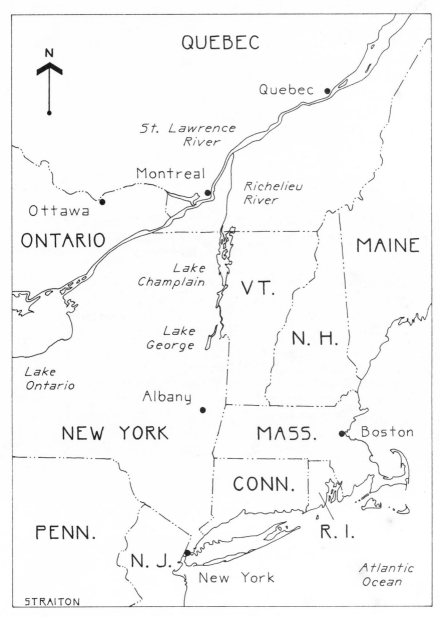

The 109 mile long Lake Champlain is the reputed home of Champ. Due to its immense size and location, Lake Champlain has been called "New England's West Coast." (courtesy: Ted Straiton)

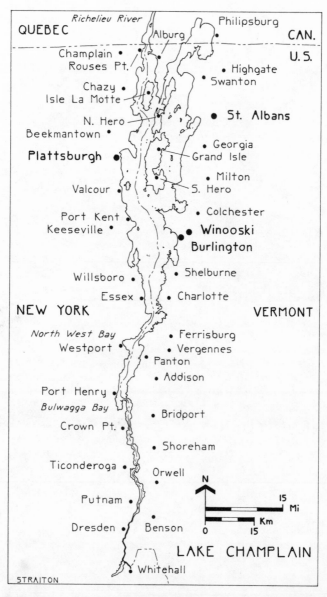

Lake Champlain's vastness — including 440 square mile water surface, 109 mile length and a maximum depth of 400 feet — could conceivably make it a massive enough haunt to harbor a colony of Loch Ness-like animals. (courtesy: Ted Straiton)

The lake's name is synonymous with Colonial American history. Historians cannot talk about one without at least mentioning the other. The 17th century saw the lake act as an avenue for exploration. The 18th and 19th centuries witnessed Lake Champlain as a roadway of war as European and American rivalries were acted out in bloody reality. During the 19th and 20th centuries the Champlain Valley gradually saw a metamorphosis in its historical legacy. The pathway of aggression evolved into a waterway of tranquility as the United States stretched its adolescent bones and expanded westward. Throughout nearly two centuries Lake Champlain was to become an increasingly important link in America's water transportation trade routes.

Today the spirit of exploration begun by the intrepid French explorer, Samuel de Champlain, in 1609, has found renewed vigor. The 1970s and 1980s have witnessed cryptozoological investigations in the lake where Samuel de Champlain's expedition recorded fauna and flora wonders and conducted cartographical surveys.

The Biology Of Lake Champlain

LAKE Champlain "is the largest of the deep, cold water and near-oligotrophic lakes in the United States with the exception of the Great Lakes."[1] The lake is located in Vermont, New York and Quebec, running north from Whitehall, New York to the Richelieu River in Quebec. The lake drains into the St. Lawrence River at Sorel, Quebec after its run along the Richelieu River. The St. Lawrence River flows into the North Atlantic Ocean. On the west of Lake Champlain lie the Adirondack Mountains of New York, and to the east is the broad, fertile plain of Vermont.

Lake Champlain as it is known today began some 8,500–10,200 years ago. Prior to that was an even larger body of water referred to as the Champlain Sea. Rather than an inland freshwater body as we have today, the Champlain Sea was an arm of the Atlantic Ocean, a marine estuary with salinity characteristics, and was originally formed by receding glacial melt waters. It was the melting glaciers, in fact, which helped account for the creation of this

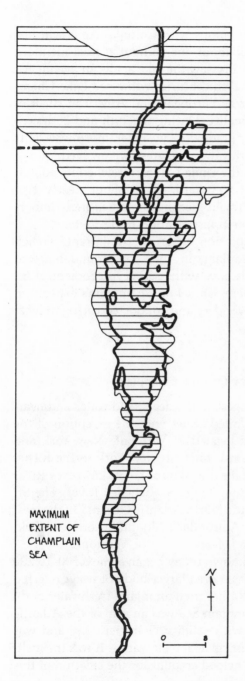

MAXIMUM
EXTENT OF
CHAMPLAIN
SEA

Lake Champlain as it is known today, began 8,500 to 10,200 years ago. Prior to that was the Champlain Sea, a marine estuary with salinity features whose maximum extent is shown in the map. (credit: Glenn E. Myer and Gerhard K. Greunding, courtesy: Monty Fischer and Anne Platt)

inland body of fresh water. According to the publication, *Limnology of Lake Champlain*, the reducing weight of the glaciers allowed some of the land to rise in elevation above that of the water level, and therefore separate the lake from the Atlantic Ocean. Subsequent fresh water input eventually diluted the saline content of the water to bring about the fresh waters of today's Lake Champlain.[2]

PHYSICAL FEATURES OF LAKE CHAMPLAIN:

Surface Water Area (square miles) 440
Island Area (square miles) 55
Total Land and Water Area (square miles) 495
Total Length (miles) 109
Maximum Width (miles) 11
Maximum Depth (feet) 400
Average Depth (feet) 64
Lake Champlain Shoreline Length (miles) 587

Lake Champlain's total shoreland population as of 1975 was 213,758 with Burlington, Vermont and Plattsburgh, New York the largest cities.[3]

Lake Champlain is also a storehouse of fish, containing over 80 different species.[4] In 1981, Anne Platt, the Executive Director of the Lake Champlain Committee, an environmental watchdog for the lake, called Lake Champlain one of the "most biologically diverse bodies of freshwater on the North American continent."[5]

Thus, Lake Champlain—immense, deep, and with ample fish-life—appears to be a comfortable environment for a community of sizeable predatory or carrion feeder animals such as Champ.

CHAPTER 2

Cryptozoology: How It
Pertains To Champ

CAN a colony of breeding Champ creatures exist? Not only is the
evidence significant enough to suggest that there does indeed
exist a breeding herd of unidentified animals in Lake Champlain,
but there also is zoological precedent. Some once-controversial
and unexpected animals of the past are today readily accepted by
the scientific community. Previously these were considered to be
myths or creatures believed by orthodox science to have become
extinct.

The scientific search for animals such as Champ, Nessie, Bigfoot, Yeti and other mystery creatures is called cryptozoology.
This is a term that was popularized by Dr. Bernard Heuvelmans
of France in the late 1950s. Dr. Heuvelmans is the acknowledged
"Father of Cryptozoology" and is the author of several books on
the subject, most notably: *In the Wake of the Sea-Serpents* and
On the Track of Unknown Animals. Cryptozoology as a term is
derived from the Greek "kryptos" meaning hidden, "zoon" meaning animal, and "logos" meaning discourse. Thus cryptozoology
is "the science of hidden animals."[6]

Recently a society was founded to promote this new science.
On January 8–9, 1982, the International Society of Cryptozoology* (ISC) was officially formed "to promote the scientific

* International Society of Cryptozoology
P.O. Box 43070
Tucson, AZ 85733 USA

Dr. Bernard Heuvelmans of France has been called the "Father of Cryptozoology" (the science of hidden animals). (courtesy: Dr. Bernard Heuvelmans)

inquiry, education, and communication among people interested in animals of unexpected form or size, or unexpected occurrence in time and space."[7] The founders' meeting was hosted by the Department of Vertebrate Zoology at the National Museum of Natural History, the Smithsonian Institution, Washington, D.C.

Cryptozoologists cite that probably the most famous of the unexpected creatures to "suddenly reappear" from extinction was the coelacanth.

In March of 1939, Professor J.C.B. Smith announced to the world the capture of a coelacanth off East London, South Africa, on December 22, 1938.[8] This steel-gray fish was caught by fishermen and brought in to an East London fish market. There it was recognized by Marjorie Courtenay-Latimer, the curator of a local museum. She then showed this fish marvel to Professor Smith.

Believed extinct for approximately 60-70 million years, the scientific world was startled when a live specimen of the coelacanth was caught on December 22, 1938 off the coast of South Africa. This specimen is in a French museum and is but one of many that have been collected over the last half century for scientific study and display. (courtesy: Jean-Pierre Sylvestre)

Not discovered until 1913, the pygmy hippopotamus is another example of a new species classified by science during the modern 20th century. (courtesy: Dr. Bernard Heuvelmans, redrawn by Rob DuBois)

Professor Smith later named the species "Latimeria chalumnae" in honor of Marjorie Courtenay-Latimer. The coelacanth is now regarded as a "living fossil," a lobe-finned ancestor to four-legged animals.

Professor Smith was so astonished by this startling discovery that he was quoted as saying, "I would hardly have been more surprised if I met a dinosaur on the street."[9] The coelacanth was believed to have died out approximately 70 million years ago. Obviously, to the delight of the scientific world, this was not the case.

Numerous other coelacanth specimens have been netted or hooked since the second one was brought up in December, 1952, off Anjouan Island of the Comoro Islands, north of Madagascar.[10] Thus, the coelacanth is the classic example of a species which was thought extinct but which bred and survived into the 20th century.

In addition, there are other once disputed creatures now known to exist. The okapi, a Miocene giraffid, was described in 1902. The pygmy hippopotamus was discovered in 1913.[11] Recently scientists have added another monstrous creature — megamouth — to the list of taxonomy.

Its scientific name is "Megachasma pelagios," known better by its common name of megamouth because of its gaping, four-foot-wide mouth. Megamouth is a new species, genus and family of shark. Of the 350 known sharks, only three are "filter-feeders," including megamouth. The 15 foot long, 1,653 pound male shark was accidentally captured in the sea off Hawaii on November 15, 1976, by a United States Navy research vessel.[12]

Leighton Taylor of the Waikiki Aquarium is one of several scientists studying the megamouth specimen. "The discovery is a timely reminder that the oceans are full of things that we don't

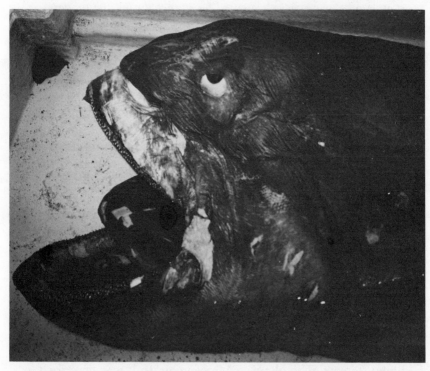

Megamouth is a 15 foot long new species, genus, and family of shark. Named after its gaping mouth, this shark was captured in the seas off Hawaii on November 15, 1976. (photo credit: L.J.V. Campagno, courtesy: Leighton Taylor, Director, Waikiki Aquarium)

Sea serpents, Champ, and other unidentified animals, are topics of investigation by cryptozoologists. This sea serpent was seen by Hans Egede, in 1734, off the South Coast of Greenland. (courtesy: Fortean Picture Library)

know anything about. Who knows what's still out there," commented Taylor, leaving smiles on the faces of the cryptozoological community who actively pursue hidden animals.[13]

The "Maybe" Monsters Of Today

DISCOVERIES such as the coelacanth, the okapi, the pygmy hippopotamus, megamouth and other zoological finds excite our imagination. They also point out how closed minded Georges Cuvier – the "Father of Paleontology" (the study of fossils and ancient life forms) – was when he stated in 1812, "There is little hope of discovering new species of large quadrapeds."[14]

Quite the contrary, Dr. Roy P. Mackal of the University of Chicago fueled enthusiasm for cryptozoological pursuit when he wrote in 1980, ". . . we are quite a long way from scraping the bottom of the barrel of zoological unknowns. The fact is that there are quite a number of areas, some large, some small, some

Another "maybe monster"—the mokele-mbembe of Central Africa. Descriptions from Congolese natives of recent sightings of this creature suggest that a small sauropod dinosaur, such as the Camarasaurus, might be living in Central Africa. (credit: David W. Miller, courtesy: Dr. Roy P. Mackal)

water, and some land, where the probability is quite high that large unidentified animals still exist waiting for our curious eyes."[15]

In his article, "What Is Cryptozoology?," Dr. Bernard Heuvelmans wrote: ". . . it would not be surprising today if we discovered an average of 7,000 new varieties of insects every year, hundreds of varieties of each of the large groups of the marine invertebrates . . . , and about a hundred varieties of fish. . . . Every year, an average of three or four amphibians, two or three reptiles, as many birds, and nearly a dozen mammals are discovered."

Therefore it would seem very possible that in that barrel of

Dr. Roy P. Mackal, center left with light cap and rifle, has lead two expeditions into the Likouala region of the Congo in search of the mokele-mbembe. Pictured here is his second expedition team in 1981. (photo credit: Marie T. Womack, courtesy: Dr. Roy P. Mackal)

Author, explorer and "Bigfoot and Yeti" researcher, Peter Byrne, with a cast of a Bigfoot footprint—1978. (courtesy: Peter Byrne)

This scalp is claimed by monks (Lamas) at Pangboche Temple, Sola Khumbu region, Nepal, to be that of a Yeti, the Abominable Snowman. According to cryptozoologist Peter Byrne, this scalp has been in the temple about 300 years. (courtesy: Peter Byrne)

zoological unknowns may hide "Champ, North America's Loch Ness Monster." Champ, too, has its "maybe monster" companions. Some of these other unknown animals which may exist are: large octopuses* reaching 150 feet or more in Bahamian waters; Mesozoic sauropod dinosaurs such as the mokele-mbembe of Central Africa; large hominids known as the Yeti in the Himalayas, the almas in the Soviet Union, the wildman in China, and Bigfoot or Sasquatch in North America. And along with these are reports of northern latitude "lake monsters" in such places as Loch Ness, Loch Morar and Loch Shiel in Scotland, as well as Lake Champlain.[17] Thus the search for "mystery or maybe monsters" of which Champ is but one, has its zoological precedent and its dedicated cryptozoological gumshoes.

---

* Dr. Forrest Wood of the Naval Oceans Systems Center in San Diego, California is leading the campaign for the plural of octopus to be octopuses rather than octopi.[16]

CHAPTER 3

Lake Champlain — North America's

Loch Ness

Without a doubt, Scotland is the most publicized home of mystery "water horses," but North America has numerous lakes that are the supposed haunt of lake denizens. Among the more likely creatures and lakes are: British Columbia's Ogopogo of Okanagan Lake; Ponik of Quebec's Lake Pohenegamook; Igopogo of Lake Simcoe, Ontario; Manipogo, the lake monster of Manitoba; the Flathead Lake Monster of Flathead Lake, Montana; and Champ of Lake Champlain.

Of all these North American monster lakes, Okanagan Lake and Lake Champlain have probably received the most serious scientific interest. However, within the last few years Lake Champlain has moved to the forefront as the focal point of most research into a North American lake monster. Thus it would appear Lake Champlain certainly does deserve the cognomen, "North America's Loch Ness."

Loch Ness And Lake Champlain — The Similarities

Loch Ness, Scotland's most famous lake, lies in the Great Glen, a wide fault-line which separates the Northern Highlands from the rest of Scotland. Loch Ness is 24 miles long and up to 1½ miles wide.[18] It is classified as an oligotrophic lake, that is, one deficient in plant nutrients — where the lower layer of cold water never becomes completely depleted of oxygen. The loch is approximately 975 feet deep at its greatest point,[19] although Adrian

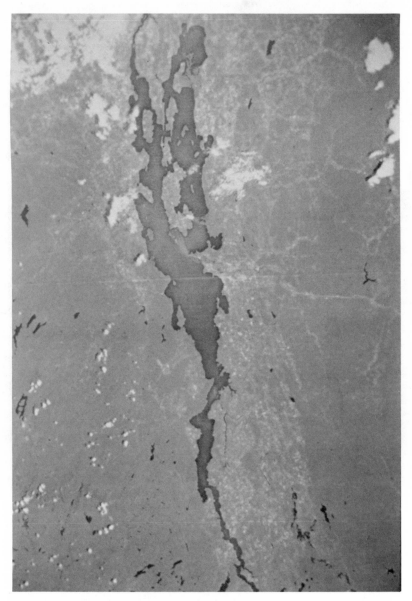

Satellite photo of Lake Champlain. (courtesy: National Aeronautics And Space Administration)

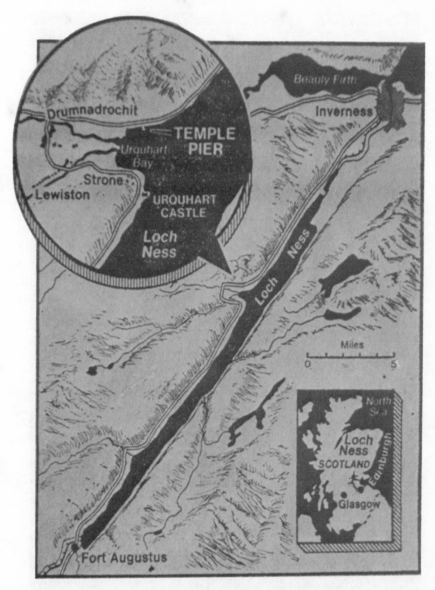

Loch Ness in Scotland's Highlands has long been renowned as the home of Nessie, the Loch Ness Monster. Today some scientists believe North America's Lake Champlain to be the habitat of similar mystery animals. (courtesy: Academy of Applied Science)

Shine of the Loch Ness and Morar Project believes this 1969 sonar reading depth figure may be inaccurate. "Echosounders calibrated for sea water over read slightly in fresh water, which may in part explain the exceptional reading," wrote Shine in 1983.[20] Nonetheless, the depth of this fabled loch over much of its length is still in excess of 700 feet.

Therefore, Loch Ness presents itself as such a formidable challenge that a journalist writing in 1961 said of it: "Nobody will ever understand Loch Ness. Its conquest will be a greater triumph than the conquest of the moon."[21]

The chart below is a brief comparison of Loch Ness and Lake Champlain. It shows some of the characteristics of both lakes that are uncannily similar.

Loch Ness

- Formed approximately 10,000 years ago
- Freshwater
- Depth — 975 feet
- Formerly an extension of Atlantic Ocean
- 52 feet above sea level
- Abundant supply of fish (the main species being salmon, brown and sea trout, arctic char, eels, pike, stickleback)
- Part of a canal system (Caledonian Canal — completed in 1822)
- Sightings of monstrous unidentified animals (approximately 3,000 recorded Nessie sightings)

Lake Champlain

- Formed approximately 8,500 to 10,200 years ago
- Freshwater
- Depth — 400 feet
- Formerly an extension of Atlantic Ocean
- 95.5 feet above sea level
- Abundant supply of fish (over 80 species — see chart in appendix)
- Part of a canal system (Champlain Canal — completed in 1823)
- Sightings of monstrous unidentified animals (over 200 recorded Champ sightings)[22]

The remains of Urquhart Castle overlooking Loch Ness. This area is the focal center for many sightings of Nessie. In a similar fashion, Bulwagga Bay, Port Henry, New York, is one of the centers of Champ sightings. It, too, has its adjacent fortifications, that of Crown Point. (photo credit: Joseph W. Zarzynski)

One of the veteran cryptozoological research organizations at Loch Ness is the Loch Ness and Morar Project whose inflatable vessel can often be observed during sonar expeditions on the loch. (photo credit: Joseph W. Zarzynski)

Colonial era Crown Point fortifications rising above Lake Champlain's Bulwagga Bay. (photo credit: Roger Bannister)

Fort Augustus, Scotland, with Loch Ness in the background, part of the Caledonian Canal completed in 1822, one year before the Champlain Canal was finished. (photo credit: Joseph W. Zarzynski)

The Champlain Canal's Lock 12, Whitehall, New York. (courtesy: Carol Greenough)

CHAPTER 4

The Evidence For Champ

THE total amassed evidence on Champ is not as extensive as that gathered at Loch Ness, since the investigation into the Champ phenomenon is only in its infancy as compared to that at Loch Ness. Still, the accumulated data on Champ is considerable and impressive: (1) Indian folklore and myths about water serpents and spirits, (2) art forms and place names, (3) eyewitness accounts of visual observations of Champ, (4) several photographs which may be of a Champ animal and (5) sonar contacts.

It would take a much larger book to thoroughly discuss and analyze all the collected Champ data. However, a brief summary of some of the data must be reviewed to give insight into the complexity of this zoological puzzle of Lake Champlain.

Indian Folklore

THERE is a multitude of Indian legends attributing water serpents to American lakes such as Lake Champlain. George R. Hamell, Senior Museum Exhibits Planner in Anthropology at the New York State Museum in Albany, New York, echoes this sentiment: "Beliefs in giant underwater serpents/dragons are universal — they are found throughout the New World — throughout North America — with numerous references in Iroquoian mythology."[23]

The Iroquois nation held hegemony over the western shore of Lake Champlain, while the Algonquin and the Abnaki controlled the eastern shore. There are several Indian names for Lake Champlain. Two of these are: "Petoubouque" (Abnaki for "The Waters that Lie Between") and "Caniaderi-Guarunte" (Iroquois for "The Door to the Country").[24]

It appears that for the Iroquois people the serpent motif was possibly an "ancestor" or "kinship" symbol. In North American Indian folklore that serpent is primarily associated with water such as streams, rivers, and possibly lakes.[25]

One of the Iroquois beliefs related to this is the Horned Serpent (the Great Horned Serpent). Their belief in the Horned Serpent

The Iroquois tribe held hegemony over the west shore of Lake Champlain. Pictured is an artist's interpretation of the Iroquois "Horned Serpent" which has similarities to some eyewitness reports of Champ's head with top protuberances, possibly Champ's ears or horns. (courtesy: Joseph MacDonough)

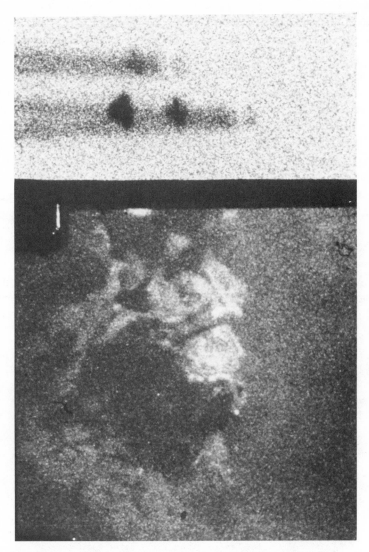

Surface Questar telescope pictures at Loch Ness by Carol Rines of the Academy of Applied Science (top) and a 1975 underwater photograph of what is believed to be Nessie's gargoyle head taken by the Academy of Applied Science (bottom) further suggest "pipes" or top protuberances off Nessie's head. Could these "pipes" be Nessie's snorkel-like breathing "horns?" (courtesy: Academy of Applied Science)

49

may link a parallelism between the Horned Serpent appearance and some eyewitnesses' accounts of the Champ animals sporting ears or horns atop their snake-like heads.

To extend this Horned Serpent and Champ similitude hypothesis another step, a 1975 subsurface photograph of what is believed to be Nessie's head taken in Urquhart Bay, Loch Ness, by the Academy of Applied Science, depicts the gargoyle-like head of Nessie with "horns." Some scientists and researchers have suggested these may be retractible horns "which may be breathing tubes."[26] A surface photograph of Loch Ness taken by Carol Rines of the Academy of Applied Science, using a camera equipped with a Questar telescope, shows "top protuberances" (pipes) which may be from a Nessie animal swimming just below the waterline. These pipes or horns may very well be part of Nessie's breathing apparatus.

Although this is very speculative, the similarities between the Iroquois Horned Serpent, Champ, and Nessie, do present an alluring comparison for future discussion.

The "Indian writings" or "petrified snakes" on the north face of Lake Champlain's Split Rock are geologically formed, but ironically depict a close resemblance to Champ's serpentine shape. (photo credit: Joseph W. Zarzynski)

This unique rock formation, Split Rock, is renowned for its "petrified snakes" geologically formed on the north side of the Gibralter-like attraction. At low water one can walk the few feet from Split Rock Point to Split Rock. (photo credit: M.P. Meaney)

The "Indian writings" or "petrified snakes" on the north side of Split Rock, located south of Essex, New York, likewise present another aspect of Indian folklore related to the Champ animals.

In his book, *The Story of Three Towns: Westport, Essex, and Willsboro, New York*, historian Morris F. Glenn calls Split Rock "probably one of the best known and most celebrated natural features on Lake Champlain." Standing 30 feet above water, patched with tree and shrub vegetation and covering an area of one-half acre, this rock is a mini-Gibralter. The promontory rock is not actually separated from the peninsula, and at low water a visitor can walk the few feet from Split Rock Point to Split Rock.

Split Rock's "Indian writings" or "petrified snakes" are not petroglyphs, but "really contorted segregations of silicates that only resemble snakes."[27] I contend that these serpentine formations were held in great reverence by the indigenous Indians because of their knowledge of Champ and their possible association to the Champ-like formations.

There is a second point pertaining to Split Rock's Indian folk-lore and Champ. Split Rock was called "Rock Regio" after an Indian chief who died there. According to Indian legend the ghost of this chief supposedly took up residence beneath the rock. "He had power over the winds and waves, and to propitiate him the Indians were accustomed to throw gifts to him as they passed in their canoes."[28] Arent Van Corlear (Van Curler), founder of Schenectady, New York, is reported to have made an "insulting gesture" toward the ghost of the Indian chief of Split Rock in 1667 while canoeing on the lake. In a 1975 letter to Mayor Erastus Corning, historian Lewis L. Tucker wrote of the incident: "According to the legend, the Indian chief was incensed by Van Curler's gesture and raised a 'great wind' which upset the canoe and caused the Dutchman to drown in 'Perou Bay' (today's Willsboro Bay in the town of Willsboro)."

Art Forms And Place Names

Art forms and place names have their pieces, too, in the Champ jigsaw puzzle.

In September, 1760, Abel Horsmer engraved on his 15¾ inch powderhorn: the British Royal Coat of Arms, two marching soldiers, a horse, an Indian, a bird in a tree, Fort Amherst and a rather large dragon-like creature.[29]

This powderhorn was first brought to my attention by Mr. Tim Titus of the Crown Point State Historic Site located on the shores of Lake Champlain. It is currently part of a private collection owned by Mr. Nathan L. Swayze of Yazoo City, Mississippi.

The dragon etched by this soldier at Crown Point is another possible link that Colonial America was aware of the Champ animals of Lake Champlain.

Place names certainly have their role in this chronicle of Champ, too. Lake Champlain's Big Snake Bay or Snake Den Harbor is located several miles north of Westport, New York. The name Big Snake Bay has several connotations, one of which suggests a direct relationship to the Champ creatures and the derivation of

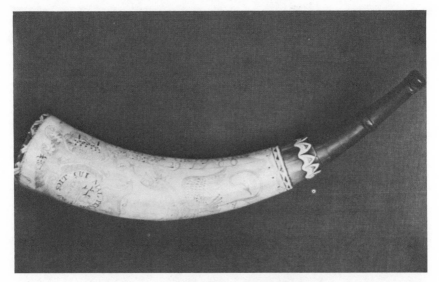

A colonial engraving from the Champlain Valley shows a dragon-like creature etched on a powderhorn — thus another possible piece of the Champ zoological jigsaw puzzle. (courtesy: Nathan L. Swayze)

this bay's name. The bay is named Big Snake Bay on the U.S. Geological Survey maps and is referred to as Snake Den Harbor on the National Ocean Survey charts. In 1978, the United States Board On Geographic Names investigated and reviewed the discrepancy in these two names. The harbor was used years ago to load slabs of granite onto barges, and reportedly there was a rattlesnake den nearby on the adjacent rock slopes.[30] The Domestic Geographic Names section recommended the bay be called Snake Den Harbor rather than Big Snake Bay.[31] Nonetheless, it is still engrossing to consider the coincidence in the name Big Snake Bay. Possibly there was something more serpentine to this bay's name than just rattlesnakes!

Eyewitness Accounts Of Visual Observations Of Champ

By far the most Champ evidence we have comes from eyewitness sightings. Over two hundred sightings of Champ are on file with

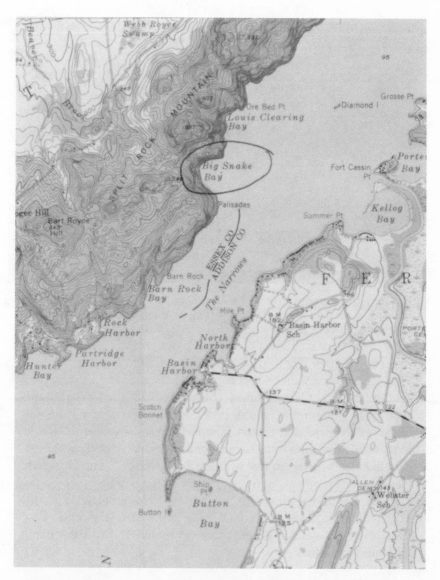

Is it coincidence or more Champ evidence that a large cove of Lake Champlain is named Big Snake Bay on a U.S. Geological Survey Map? (courtesy: U.S. Geological Survey, Washington, D.C.)

the Lake Champlain Phenomena Investigation. Although eye-witness sightings can be plagued by bias, misinterpretation, problems of communication and many other twists, the observers still have a distinct advantage in that they were present, and they saw.

Father J. A. Carruth in his booklet, *Loch Ness and Its Monster*, says of reliable Loch Ness witnesses, "Unless all these people were lying, and lying in the same way — people who have never seen one another — we are forced to accept their testimony as genuine, for it is impossible for them all to have been deceived in the same way." This statement applies to the Lake Champlain sightings as well.

Undoubtedly many early Champ sightings have yet to be discovered, awaiting further archival research in all the newspaper morgues, museums, and libraries that saturate the Champlain

Due to the many Champ sightings around Bulwagga Bay, the residents of Port Henry, New York, have erected a roadside board commemorating eyewitness sightings. (photo credit: Joseph W. Zarzynski)

Valley. However, of those more than two hundred sightings which have been documented, one is impressed with the quality and detail of account. Nonetheless, this is just a fraction of those sightings that have actually taken place. Many sightings have been kept confidential for fear of ridicule or ostracism. Fortunately, a more positive willingness to discuss Champ sightings has been created over the years, and more and more individuals are "coming out of the closet" to tell their story.

Yet even those recorded sightings must be scrutinized for accuracy. Some of the sightings of the late 19th century quite possibly were products of imaginative reporters or editors simply trying to sell a good story.

It should be re-emphasized that the research and field work on Lake Champlain is still very much in the formative stages, while Loch Ness has been the most studied lake in the world pertaining

As the unofficial mascot of Port Henry, New York, this rendition of Champ was painted by Bonnie Clonan. (photo credit: Roger Bannister)

to its mysterious inhabitants. With sightings of Nessie dating back to 565 A.D., public and scientific infatuation with the Ness phenomenon finally began in 1933. The construction of a new road on the north shore of Loch Ness, a visionary newspaper editor and an inquisitive public half a century ago, combined to create a sudden surge of research and investigation. With this headstart at Loch Ness, scientists there are able to base their hypotheses on more data than we have from Lake Champlain. Nevertheless, some statements and possible conclusions may be offered from the Champ information available.

The "Champ Photographs"

PHOTOGRAPHS and film footage of Champ are rare. This is certainly not the case at Loch Ness.

In 1976, in his book, *The Monsters of Loch Ness*, Dr. Mackal wrote that: "Hundreds of still photographs have been made of Loch Ness surface disturbances, but disappointingly most can easily be identified as pictures of logs, birds, etc." In that book, Dr. Mackal claimed to know of only 22 film sequences from Loch Ness of what might be a Nessie creature. Since that time there have been other still photographs and film footage reportedly shot at Loch Ness. Besides this surface photography, the American-based and much respected Academy of Applied Science from Boston, Massachusetts and Concord, New Hampshire, has acquired several subsurface photographs during their long tenure at the loch in the 1970s and '80s.

Unfortunately, to date, reported still photographs and film sequences at Lake Champlain are not that prolific. There are several reasons for this. First, Loch Ness has generated an atmosphere that encourages residents, visitors and researchers to carry a camera and to be prepared to use it. This habit is just now starting to be practiced at Lake Champlain. Second, there have been many scientific search groups at Loch Ness, there for the primary purpose of attempting to get that definitive photographic evidence of the Nessie animals. Among some of those organized

That Sea Serpent

AS IT IS SUPPOSED TO HAVE APPEARED TO TWO
OF OUR CITIZENS.

The late 19th century was a flap period for numerous Champ sightings and interest in "That Sea Serpent" of Lake Champlain as characterized by this woodcut print from the Swanton, Vermont Courier — October 7, 1882 by T. Tobin. (courtesy: O'Shea Publishing)

teams have been: the Sir Edward Mountain Expedition (1934), the Loch Ness Investigation Bureau (the 1960s), the Academy of Applied Science (1970s–1980s), National Geographic Society (1976), the Loch Ness and Morar Project (1970s–1980s), and "Operation Deepscan" (1986 & 1987). Loch Ness has also seen its dedicated individual Nessie investigators: Tim Dinsdale, Nick Witchell, Ivor Newby, F.W. Holiday, Torquil MacLeod, Rip Hepple, Tony Healy, Jim Hogan, Holly Arnold and many others.[32]

Lake Champlain has only two organized cryptozoological groups for on going investigation, the Lake Champlain Phenomena Investigation and Wind & Whalebone Media Productions. Increasingly, more and more people are showing a forthright and hearty interest in Champ and are conducting their own independent camera watches. In a very progressive move, in 1982, the Vermont Department of Fish and Game equipped its large research vessel and some of its lake wardens with cameras, and instructions to take photographs of anything that "looks like it might be 'Champ.' "[33]

Another factor contributing to the abundance of Nessie photographs is that Loch Ness is more conducive to surface camera surveillance. Its shoreline does not meander as much as that of Lake Champlain. Loch Ness' route A82 and route B852 (General Wade's old military road) run mostly along the Loch Ness shoreline. Much of these two roads at Loch Ness are elevated, thus giving unobstructed views of the 24 mile long loch. Also, every

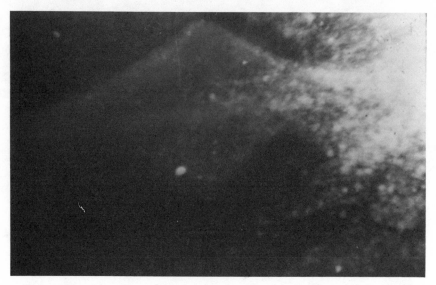

This 1972 underwater photograph taken by the Academy of Applied Science shows a diamond-shaped appendage or flipper of Nessie. Acquired by elapsed time photography during simultaneous sonar tracking, this computer enhanced photograph is considered to be one of the best pieces of evidence to date on Nessie. (courtesy: Academy of Applied Science)

More photographic evidence on aquatic mystery animals has been collected at Loch Ness than Lake Champlain, in part due to a half century of scientific expeditioning at Scotland's most famous loch. Dr. Robert Rines (left), Marty Klein (center) and Tim Dinsdale (right) launch a side-scan sonar towfish at Loch Ness in 1970. (© Klein Associates, Inc., courtesy: Klein Associates, Inc.)

Scott Hill (left), Jim Kennard (center), and Joseph Zarzynski (right) of Lake Champlain Phenomena Investigation, check a sonar unit at Lake Champlain in 1981. (photo credit: M.P. Meaney)

few miles "laybys" are found on these two roads where a vehicle can pull off to allow its passengers to peruse the waters of the magical loch in search of its evasive beasties. Lake Champlain does not have this roadway or topographic luxury.

Nonetheless, I know of 12 people who claim to have Champ photographs, at least two who feel they may possibly have Champ on motion picture film, and one person who claims he has videography of Champ. Of these, I have seen eight people's photographs, one motion picture sequence, and the videotape. Three of these still photographs have been published in the August, 1982, issue of *Life* magazine. However, in my opinion, the classic Champ photograph is still the 1977 Mansi photo.

The Mansi Photograph

Oɴ July 5th, 1977, a typical summer's day, Anthony and Sandra Mansi (then engaged) journeyed by car from the Vergennes, Vermont area north to St. Albans, Vermont. Sandra and Anthony had two children with them from Sandra's previous marriage. They had spent the night with Sandra's relative near Vergennes, and now found themselves at a picturesque lakeside field somewhere in the St. Albans vicinity. Enjoying the splendid Champlain Valley scenery, they parked their vehicle near the lake and watched the two children wade in the shallows just offshore. It was a scene quite familiar to sightseers of Lake Champlain. This

Probably the best surface photograph of Champ was taken by Sandra Mansi on July 5, 1977. Sandra Mansi (right), Anthony Mansi (left), and Joseph W. Zarzynski (center) at Lake Champlain in 1980. (photo credit: Richard Cowperthwait)

idyllic recreation period was suddenly shattered as the dark head and neck of a "dinosaur" reared out of the surface of the lake. Anthony slid a Kodak Instamatic camera from his sweater pocket and handed it to Sandra. Fortunately, Sandra had enough presence to snap a photograph of this awesome animal while Anthony helped the unknowing children onto shore.

The Mansis estimate their sighting lasted approximately four to five minutes, and figure their distance from the object at about 150 feet. Sandra later testified that the "dinosaur's" head and neck was approximately six feet out from the water's surface and "from neck to end was 12 feet to 15 feet."[34]

Sandra Mansi took only the one photograph, and then the family returned to their parked car.

"We wondered if we should go to the police," stated Anthony Mansi. "But then we figured, if we walk into the police station and say, 'We just saw a monster in the water,' they'd laugh at us."

When the film was developed the Mansis were elated at what was pictured in the color photograph. However, ". . . we didn't want to be called a bunch of nuts, so we just threw it in the photo album," noted Anthony Mansi.[35]

In the autumn of 1979, the Mansis, with an associate of theirs, Roy Kappeler, contacted Dr. Philip Reines at the State University of New York at Plattsburgh. Dr. Reines, a professor of communications, then contacted me. We were able to get the Mansi photograph examined by Dr. George Zug of the Department of Vertebrate Zoology at the National Museum of Natural History, Smithsonian Institution, Washington, D.C.

In 1980, Dr. Zug wrote: "The Mansi photograph is fascinating and quite good considering the circumstances under which it was taken. Unfortunately, I can offer no unequivocal identification. . . . Certainly all our examinations cast no doubts on the authenticity of their photograph and report."[36]

I then contacted Dr. Roy P. Mackal of the University of Chicago who sent the Mansi photograph to Mr. J. Richard Greenwell of the University of Arizona. Through Mr. Greenwell's ministrations the photograph was studied by the Optical Sciences Center

*The 1977 Mansi photograph shows what may be the head/neck
(center), hump (right) and an appendage (left) of Champ at a range
of approximately 150 feet from the camera lens. The photograph was
first released to the public in the* New York Times *on June 30, 1981.
(© 1981 Sandra Mansi — all rights reserved Gamma Liaison)*

at the University of Arizona. Work on the photograph was coordinated under the direction of Dr. B. Roy Frieden of the Optical
Sciences Center. Much of the Frieden analysis on the Mansi
photograph was completed at Kitt Peak National Observatory in
Arizona.

Dr. B. Roy Frieden stated in his "Interim Report/Lake Champlain 'Monster' Photograph" (April 30, 1981) that "the photo does
not appear to be a montage or a superposition of any kind" and
thus no evidence of a laboratory hoax.

Mr. Alan Neigher, the Westport, Connecticut attorney repre-
senting the Mansi family, said in 1981 of his clients that they
"could no more have constructed such a hoax than put a satellite
in orbit."[37]

This April, 1934 photograph of Nessie dubbed the "Surgeons photograph" was taken by Lt. Col. Robert K. Wilson, M.D. Note the similarities of the serpentine head and neck in the Mansi photograph with this now classic Surgeons photograph. (credit: Associated Newpapers Group, Ltd; acknowledge: London Daily Mail)

However, Dr. Frieden was bothered by the possible presence of a sandbar in the Mansi photograph. ". . . if it is a sandbar then there is a distinct possibility that the object was put there by someone. . . ."[38] By "object," Dr. Frieden was referring to the "monster" and the possibility of a hoax by someone.

Dr. Paul H. LeBlond, an oceanographer from the University of British Columbia and a member of the Board of Directors of the International Society of Cryptozoology, wrote in 1982 after his analysis of the Mansi print: "Although it might be argued that this feature reveals the presence of a relatively shallow sandy area in that part of the lake, this hypothesis is inconsistent with the behavior of the waves travelling over that area." Thus, his analysis refutes the likelihood of a planted model on a shallow sandbar that Dr. Frieden addressed.

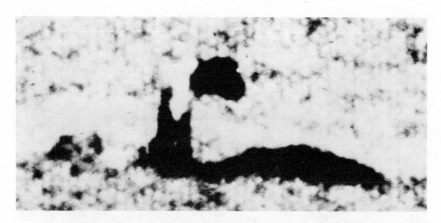

This electronic heavy enhancement of the Mansi photograph demonstrates "that the monster's 'back' and 'head' are connected (not clearly visible to the eye in the original print)." However, the computer enhancement "could not resolve facial features because the head was heavily shadowed." (© ISC, courtesy: J. Richard Greenwell and the ISC)

This reverse contrast image of the Mansi photograph, like the electronic heavy enhancement, was conducted by Dr. B. Roy Frieden of the University of Arizona's Optical Sciences Center and Kitt Peak National Observatory scientists. (© ISC, courtesy: J. Richard Greenwell and the ISC)

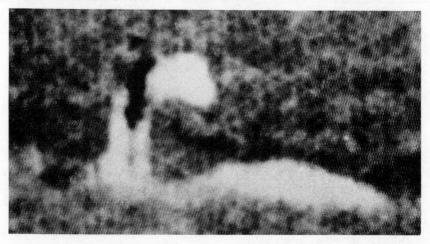

Dr. LeBlond's dynamics analysis of the Mansi photograph using "the general appearance of the water surface" in the photograph, stated "it may be possible to estimate the length of waves seen thereon, and hence to use the latter as a scale with which to compare objects of uncertain dimensions."

Thus, from the LeBlond analysis, the water-line dimension of "Champ" in the Mansi photograph "ranges from an extreme lower bound of 4.8 m to an extreme upper bound of 17.2 m."

Dr. LeBlond completed his analysis report by writing: "The inescapable conclusion, nevertheless, is that the object seen in the Mansi photograph is of considerable size. The visual estimate given by Mr. Mansi (15 to 20 feet: 4.6 to 6.1 meters at the water-line) falls within the lower part of the length range estimated here, and provides independent confirmation of this conclusion."[39]

The Summer, 1982 issue of *The ISC Newsletter*, published by the International Society of Cryptozoology, stated that Dr. Frieden's analysis and the photograph's image enhancements "did demonstrate that the monster's 'back' and 'head' are connected (not clearly visible to the eye in the original print). . . ." The enhancement however "could not resolve the facial features because the head was heavily shadowed."

The 1977 Mansi photograph was eventually released to the public via the *New York Times* on June 30, 1981 (black and white version) and the color print of the Mansi photograph first appeared in *Time* and *Macleans* magazines on July 13, 1981.

Although the negative of the Mansi print has been lost and the Mansi family can not exactly recall on which stretch of Lake Champlain's 587 miles of shoreline they took their now classic photograph, I personally consider it to be the single best piece of evidence on Champ. Work continues by the L.C.P.I., with assistance from Mr. Ted Straiton of Leominster, Massachusetts, to relocate the Mansi site. The difficulties of time elapsed, geography, and the fact that the Mansis were a Connecticut family in unfamiliar territory, offer stiff obstacles in this search.

Now, 11 years after the Mansi photo was snapped, further review of their photograph has taken place. Mr. Richard D. Smith,

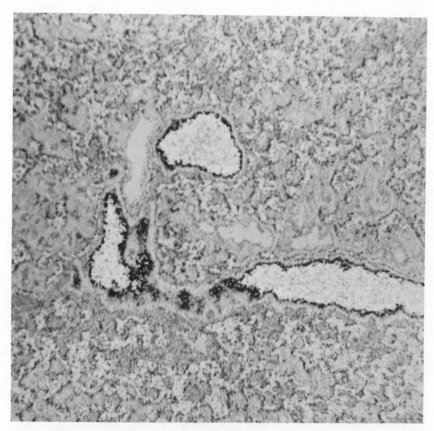

Visually artistic and attractive, this electronic reproduction is a false-color image of the Mansi photograph done during a photographic analysis session at Kitt Peak National Observatory in Arizona. (© ISC, courtesy: J. Richard Greenwell and the ISC)

a filmmaker and head of Wind & Whalebone Media Productions in New Jersey, is producing a documentary on cryptozoology. He has interviewed Sandra Mansi and studied the Mansi photograph. In 1983 he wrote:

It's quite important to note that the major aspects of Sandra Mansi's accounts are thoroughly consistent with the majority of eyewitness reports of similar animals in similar lakes, particularly at Loch Ness, Scotland. . . . there is to my eye a real sense of life and movement to the object in the Mansi photo . . . a true muscularity and tension apparent in the head/neck poised over the humped body.

As a photographer and filmmaker, I can speak with some authority as to what it would take to fake a picture of this sort. Assuming the remote possibility that the Mansi photo is a fraud, it would require fabrication of an excellent, full-sized model (highly expensive in terms of expertise and materials) which would have to be smuggled out to Champlain or another lake, there assembled or inflated, and successfully maneuvered around out in the water (most difficult, especially with a slight wind blowing), the whole thing accomplished without being seen or the slightest leak in security (unlikely).

Here, I am anticipating criticisms of "oh, everybody knows how they do special effects in the movies these days" or "it would be simple just to . . . " etc. It would not be simple. And besides being horribly expensive, virtually all special effects work done in the movies today involves miniature models and optical printing techniques. As noted elsewhere, the Frieden and LeBlond analyses eliminate miniatures or trick photography.[40]

Gradually, people are becoming more cognizant of Champ's probable existence and, like those residents and visitors to Loch Ness, are now sporting cameras in the hopes of getting that undisputable photographic evidence toward Champ's existence.

Sonar Evidence

Sonar technology has been deployed at both Loch Ness and Lake Champlain for cryptozoological purposes. Sonar is the technique of sending sound pulses through the water and measuring the time lapsed before the echo returns. The harder the mass of the object, the stronger the echo. Through sophisticated electronics the echoes are computed and displayed on either screen or paper.

Sonar technology received an impetus from World War II when it was developed for tracking submarines. That same appli-

An artist's concept of Klein Side-Scan Sonar technique. This type of side-scan sonar has been deployed at both Loch Ness and Lake Champlain on cryptozoological expeditions. (© Klein Associates, Inc., courtesy: Klein Associates, Inc.)

cation has been used successfully at Loch Ness and to a more limited degree at Lake Champlain.

On December 2, 1954, the vessel, *Rival III*, picked up a sonar
target in Loch Ness on its echo sounder chart[41] — a large object
was reported at a depth of 480 feet.[42]

Since that time, numerous commercial vessels have reported
strange sonar contacts, and various researchers have undertaken
sonar searches at Loch Ness: the University of Birmingham; the
Loch Ness Investigation Bureau; the Academy of Applied Science;
the Loch Ness and Morar Project; Jim Hogan and Caley Cruisers,

*Klein Associates, Inc., of Salem, New Hampshire, has produced side-
scan sonar units since 1968. Klein sonar units have been used to
search for shipwrecks, sunken aircraft, and "monsters," and have been
deployed during many other underwater survey projects. In 1987
Klein Associates, Inc. participated in "Project 'Champ' Carcass," an
underwater search at Lake Champlain looking for a carcass of
Champ. (photo credit: Joseph W. Zarzynski)*

Ltd.; Klein Associates, Inc.; Iscan, Inc.; Lowrance Electronics; and many others. To summarize this sonar search at Loch Ness, Dr. Robert H. Rines of The Academy of Applied Science wrote: ". . . striking, however, is the repeatability in the hands of different researchers, at different times, with widely different sonar equipment, of the same-dimensioned and shaped echo characteristics from extremely large moving targets in the loch—all quite distinctive from boat, wake and fish echoes."[43]

The man who has probably conducted the greatest amount of sophisticated sonar work at Lake Champlain is Jim Kennard, President of the Rochester Engineering Laboratories—a marine search and sonar business—in Fairport, New York, and now employed by Kodak of Rochester, New York. He is an associate of and technical advisor to the Lake Champlain Phenomena Investigation, and in the late 1970s and early 1980s donated his boat and side-scan sonar for the Champ search.

Working primarily with his assistant, Scott Hill, Mr. Kennard has spent over 200 hours of sonar running time on Lake Champlain. During part of that time I was able to assist in the underwater sonar search for Champ, looking for either the physical remains of a carcass or a living Champ target. During these searches we have recorded several shipwrecks, a valuable byproduct of our Champ investigation.

However, the most productive moment of our Champ-related sonar expedition came when a possible Champ sonar target was picked up on June 3, 1979, in Whallon Bay on the New York State side of Lake Champlain. Side-scan sonar can be used in either towing fashion or stationary mode. In this case the towfish was suspended from the boat, when a large moving object was picked up in Whallon Bay at a depth of about 175 feet. Jim Kennard was quoted as explaining these as "curious readings," and possibly from a large body, although they may have come from a large school of fish.[44]

Besides the side-scan sonar (100 kHz), the L.C.P.I. has used a second type of sonar in the lake—a modified Raytheon DE725C (200 kHz) affixed to a metal tripod and placed on the lake's floor

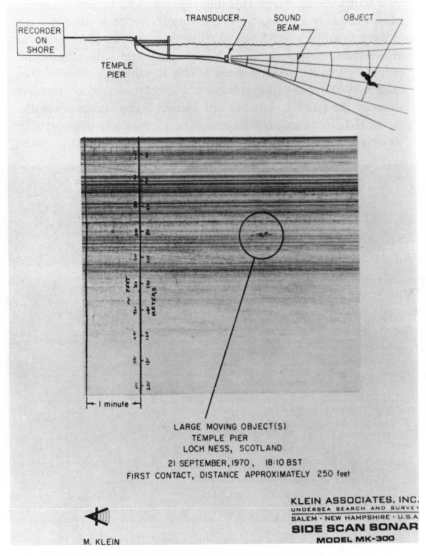

LARGE MOVING OBJECT(S)
TEMPLE PIER
LOCH NESS, SCOTLAND
21 SEPTEMBER, 1970 , 18:10 BST
FIRST CONTACT, DISTANCE APPROXIMATELY 250 feet

KLEIN ASSOCIATES, INC.
UNDERSEA SEARCH AND SURVEY
SALEM · NEW HAMPSHIRE · U.S.A.
SIDE SCAN SONAR
MODEL MK-300

M. KLEIN

Marty Klein's Klein Associates, Inc. working with the Academy of Applied Science, is but one of several organizations and individuals that have tracked large moving objects in Loch Ness using sonar. (courtesy: Klein Associates, Inc.)

by a scuba diving team. This unit was financed by Jim Kennard, Mayor Erastus Corning II of Albany, New York, and myself. (Mayor Corning was Mayor of Albany from 1942–1983, and was also a longtime patron of both Loch Ness and Lake Champlain cryptozoological investigations.) The Raytheon unit was first used in 1980 in Lake Champlain and has been used most summers since by the L.C.P.I., but has not met with any concrete results.

The L.C.P.I. has encouraged Lake Champlain boaters with sonar apparatus to report any anomalies that may possibly stem

The object in this sonar trace was nicknamed "The Average Plesiosaur," after the prehistoric reptile that has been a candidate for the identity of the "Loch Ness Monster." The object, about 10 meters long, was detected in about 100 meters of water off Fort Augustus. (© Klein Associates, Inc. and the Academy of Applied Science, courtesy: Klein Associates, Inc.)

Garry Kozak (seated behind sonar controls) and Joseph W. Zarzynski were part of a 1987 six day bottom search at Lake Champlain to find a carcass of a Champ animal. The expedition, called "Project 'Champ' Carcass," was coordinated by the L.C.P.I. and used a side-scan sonar and an underwater robot with a video camera called a ROV. Three businesses — Klein Associates, Inc., Kaselaan & D'Angelo Associates, Inc., and Vermont Dive Charter — donated gear to the L.C.P.I. for this high technology Champ carcass search. (photo credit: M.P. Meaney)

from a Champ animal. On May 1, 1982, Mr. Raymond W. Sargent of North Hero, Vermont, had a sighting of a dark brown or black creature with "18 inches to 24 inches of head and neck above surface." Mr. Sargent was under way in his houseboat at the time of his sighting and was approximately 150 yards from the unidentified animal.

"Upon passing over the sighting, my sonar depth sounder became erratic showing a blip at every digit on the scale markings," wrote Mr. Sargent.[45] "This anomaly appeared for approximately 15 to 30 seconds whereupon the instrument returned to normal operation and has functioned fine ever since."[46]

Mr. Marty Klein, President of Klein Associates, Inc., examined the written testimony of Raymond W. Sargent. Marty Klein is an

The Lake Champlain Phenomena Investigation has used both side-scan sonar and this Raytheon DE725C sonar unit — affixed on a tripod and deployed from the bottom of Lake Champlain — during its sonar search for Champ. The sonar tripod is set into position by a scuba team directed by Joseph W. Zarzynski (pictured). (photo credit: M.P. Meaney)

acknowledged world authority on sonar, and his Klein Side-Scan Sonar units are considered to be one of the finest commercially produced sonar units in the world. Klein Side-Scan Sonar units have been deployed on Loch Ness, as well as Lake Champlain, and have located many important shipwrecks including the H.M.S. EDINBURGH, the William K. Vanderbilt luxury yacht, ALVA, War of 1812 schooners, SCOURGE and HAMILTON, and hundreds of other historic shipwrecks. Klein units are also put into action in oceanographic research and exploration.

After studying the Sargent testimony, Klein wrote to me on

Joseph W. Zarzynski adjusting a Raytheon sonar unit during Champ field work. Zarzynski believes sonar use at Lake Champlain should be of intermittent usage so as not to develop a sonar pattern that might be detected by Champ animals. (photo credit: M.P. Meaney)

Longtime Nessie and Champ enthusiast, Mayor Erastus Corning II of Albany, New York, donated money toward the purchase of the Raytheon sonar unit used by the Lake Champlain Phenomena Investigation. Corning died in 1983 at the age of 73, after being Mayor of New York State's capital for 41 years. (courtesy: Mayor Thomas M. Whalen III of Albany, New York)

November 3, 1982, saying: "The fact that the unit was flashing across the entire scale can mean some noise sources in the area such as an outboard or a possible electrical malfunction. Of course, it could also be a big chirp from Champ. I don't think we can, unfortunately, draw any scientific conclusion."

Sonar use on Lake Champlain should and will continue as a means for data collection on Champ. Intermittent usage should be the cardinal law with these types of sonar probes in order to prevent a pattern.

"It could be the sonar signals plus the noise from the boat sends them swimming out of range,"[47] expressed Mr. Clive Cussler, critically acclaimed author of such books as *Raise the Titanic, Pacific Vortex*, and others. Mr. Cussler is also an internationally respected underwater archaeologist who, in 1983, using side-scan sonar, located the wreck of the LEXINGTON (a passenger-cargo ship built by Cornelius Vanderbilt in 1835) at the bottom of Long Island Sound.

In 1982, the Loch Ness and Morar Project conducted an in depth sonar scan at Loch Ness, picking up 40 sonar targets of Nessie-like animals. It is my belief that intensive sonar work at Lake Champlain — oriented specifically at cryptozoology and focused towards deep water searches — may obtain similar results as those of Loch Ness which produced "data consistent with the presence of large animals."[48]

Champ On Land

DENIZENS of the deep have been reported on land, too.

"It is not widely known that large creatures have been seen on the banks and even on the roads surrounding Loch Ness, although this has happened about a dozen times on record," wrote Nicholas Witchell in his booklet, *Loch Ness and the Monster*. And there have been at least two sightings of Ogopogo, the Okanagan Lake mystery animal, on land.[49]

On September 27, 1894, the *Essex County Republican* newspaper of upstate New York printed a story about a land sighting of "the Champlain Sea Serpent." Luther Hager, Tim Miller, Frank Dominy and Ephraim Allen saw the sea serpent at Cumberland Head, Plattsburgh, New York. "It caused a great commotion in the water . . . and came toward the shore and out of the water six feet or more upon the land."

In the spring of 1961, Thomas E. Morse reported a Champ sighting in North West Bay, Westport, New York.

"When first seen it appeared as a massive gunmetal gray approx. 18 inches wide cable on the shore and out into the lake," penned Mr. Morse on September 20, 1980. "It appeared to be a monstrous eel with white teeth that raked rearward in the mouth." Morse's sighting was from a car while driving adjacent to, and overlooking, the bay. He reports the creature, while on the shore, lifted its head a full four feet, possibly because of the car noise.

Rumors of other Champ sightings on land have circulated throughout the Champlain Valley. If there is any accuracy to these land sightings at Loch Ness, Lake Champlain and other aquatic monster haunts, it would be pure speculation to conjecture as to why these massive animals made their terrestrial treks. One hypothesis, however, is that they are mammals, and thus have amphibious tendencies. Their land sojourns may somehow be associated with hereditary impulse "since all known aquatic mammals are derived from land-dwelling forms."[50]

Why No Champ Carcass?

PEOPLE often ask: "If these Champ animals do exist, why no Champ carcass?"

The most scientifically reasoned reply to that comes from Dr. George Zug of the Smithsonian Institution in Washington, D.C., as quoted from the August, 1983 edition of *Champ Channels*:

Dr. Zug in a paper delivered at the August 29, 1981, "Does Champ Exist?" Seminar in Shelburne, Vermont, suggested these possible arguments why a Champ carcass washing ashore would be a rarity.

• If Champ were like dolphins, most deaths would occur in the winter and thus the probability of a stranding would be "infinitesimal."

Like sea serpents, Nessie and Champ have been observed both in water and on land. This drawing is by an artist based on a sighting by six 12 year old girls of a sea monster seen on the beach and in the sea at Barmouth, Gwynedd, Wales, on March 2, 1975. (courtesy: Fortean Picture Library)

(Generally, Lake Champlain, unlike Loch Ness, Scotland, does freeze over, although there have been several years in which Lake Champlain did not completely ice over.)

• If a carcass did float ashore the likelihood of its discovery would be minimal. There are no regular patrols of the lake's shores as there are for reporting the strandings of all cetaceans on our ocean coasts to allow the Smithsonian's marine mammalogist to accurately record cetacean strandings. (Lake Champlain has 587 miles of shoreline.)

• Lake Champlain does not "have wide sandy beaches to toss a carcass on nor regular tidal surges to leave the carcass high and dry."

• "Certainly the absence of a stranded carcass does not negate the possible existence of large aquatic animals; however the absence does not support the existence of such creatures either," suggested Dr. Zug.

CHAPTER 5

Champ And Americana

CHAMP is gradually obtaining its proper nook in American heritage. From time to time famous and eminent American personalities have in one form oɪ fashion been associated with the Champ story.

The earliest chapter of this would be the Champ sighting attributed to the daring French explorer Samuel de Champlain.

Marjorie L. Porter in her article, "The Champlain Monster," in the Summer, 1970 issue of *Vermont Life* magazine, wrote: "After all, the early Lake Champlain tourist, Samuel de Champlain, in July of 1609 reported and recorded his impression of a serpent-like creature about twenty feet long, as thick through as a barrel and with a head shaped like a horse."

In *The Works of Samuel de Champlain* edited by H. P. Biggar, Champlain reported he saw some "Chaousarou" about "five feet long, which were as big as my thigh, and had a head as large as my two fists, with a snout two feet and a half long, and a double row of very sharp, dangerous teeth."

Thus, what did Champlain actually see? Why did the historian Marjorie L. Porter, now deceased, write that the valiant explorer observed a 20 foot long serpent-like creature? Even though this sighting is currently undergoing historical re-examination to ascertain its role in the Champ chronicles, it is noteworthy to cite that Champlain may have seen a Champ animal, or his sighting may have been nothing more than a large gar pike or lake sturgeon. The debate on this point still persists!

According to the *Whitehall Times* of November 5, 1873, the famed circus magnate, P. T. Barnum, is supposed to have offered a $50,000 reward for the Lake Champlain Serpent. In 1887, Barnum once again offered a colossal sum of money for the creature. This time his reward was $20,000 for the sea serpent, dead or alive.[51]

1873 also had Thomas Nast, the popular caricaturist of *Harper's Weekly*, drawing sketches of the noble Champlain Serpent

In the late 19th century, circus magnate, P.T. Barnum, offered enormous sums of money for the Lake Champlain sea serpent. (credit: Joseph MacDonough)

while lecturing in Whitehall, New York. Nast entertained his audience as he did "draw forth from the bottom of Lake Champlain the hideous form of the elongated monster."[52]

W. Douglas Burden of Charlotte, Vermont, which is located on the shores of Lake Champlain, was for most of his eight decades a writer, explorer, naturalist and environmentalist. He cofounded Marineland on the east coast of Florida in 1938 and was president of that aquarium for a quarter of a century. He was also an honorary trustee of the American Museum of Natural History and made two trips around the world to collect specimens for the museum. His credits likewise include a 1928–1929 film he made about the Ojibway Indians called "The Silent Enemy."[53]

Famed naturalist, W. Douglas Burden (pictured here in 1960), was at home in any environment. In 1926 Burden brought back to the United States several specimens of the Komodo dragon (Varanus komodoensis). Ironically, Burden lived for many years on the shores of Lake Champlain at Charlotte, Vermont during an age when Champ interest was just beginning to mount. (courtesy: Mrs. Jeanne Bostwick)

In 1873, the popular American caricaturist, Thomas Nast, drew a sketch of the Lake Champlain Sea Serpent while lecturing in White-hall, New York. (credit: Macculloch Hall Historical Museum, Morris-town, N.J.)

First discovered in 1912, the Komodo lizards now number about 5,000–7,000 throughout its range. Found on Komodo and other nearby islands of the Lesser Sunda group, east of Java, these sinister looking creatures look like they should have vanished with the dinosaur. (credit: Rob DuBois)

He is probably most remembered, however, for the Burden Expedition of 1926 to the island of Komodo, now part of Indonesia, to look for the "Komodo dragons." The existence of these giant lizards was first discovered by science in 1912. His expedition returned to the United States with several specimens of these monitor lizards. The Komodo dragon (Varanus komodoensis) was further described in his book, *Dragon Lizards of Komodo* (1927).

Today we can only ponder if Burden were still alive, with all this great Champ attention, would his exploring zest be tested by the zoological mystery, Champ, at his own doorstep? I would think so!

Another dedicated naturalist and contemporary of W. Douglas Burden, who may have been linked with a scientific search for Champ, was Dr. William Beebe.

In 1929, newspaper reports stated that the famed bathysphere explorer would search for the sea serpent of Lake Champlain.

At least two upstate New York newpapers — the *Albany Times Union*, July 21, 1929, and *The Saratogian*, July 24, 1929 — published articles indicating that Dr. Beebe would lead such an expedition. These articles stated that the expedition would even include the use of a submarine and an airplane.

Dr. Beebe was an indefatigable scientific pioneer. He was the

In 1929, newspaper articles indicated that the famous explorer and scientist, Dr. William Beebe, would lead an expedition in search of the Lake Champlain Sea Serpent. Was this rumor or was there any factual basis behind these reports? (© New York Zoological Society)

author of more than a score of books and led more than sixty scientific expeditions to study wildlife.

However, did Beebe ever conduct such an expedition at Lake Champlain? We're not sure. Possibly this was just a case of "name dropping" or wishful thinking.

Dr. Beebe's wife, Mrs. Elswyth Beebe, wrote to me on November 14, 1982, about this possibility:

. . . I am quite sure that he was not very much involved with the Lake Champlain Monster, tho of course the mere idea of such a neighbor would have delighted him. . . . I am sure he would have become fascinated at the idea of any close approach to any such subject.

CHAPTER 6

The Search

BEFORE discussing the search at Lake Champlain it is necessary to briefly give background about science's pursuit of Nessie.

Although reports of Nessie date back to St. Columba's sighting in 565 A.D., 1933 marked the modern interest in Nessie as a "monster." As briefly referred to earlier, the new motor road, A82, further exposed the loch to outsiders. A sighting reported by a local newspaper, the *Inverness Courier*, printed on May 2, 1933, stimulated the world's interest as it called attention to the monster. According to historical accounts, that article, written by Alex Campbell, the loch's water bailiff and a local correspondent for the *Inverness Courier*, did not initially refer to the water animal as a monster. Dr. Evan Barron, the newspaper's editor, read the report and said, "Well, if it's as big as Campbell says it is, we can't just call it a creature. It must be a real monster." And thus a zoological mystery became a popular legend.

The legend of Nessie has been doggedly pursued for half a century. In the summer of 1934 the first serious expedition was launched by Sir Edward Mountain, an insurance king, with a team of twenty loch watchers. It was not until 1961 that another organized expedition inspected the peat-stained waters of majestic Loch Ness. This group, the Loch Ness Investigation Bureau, utilized long range camera gear during the summer to try to get the definitive photograph of Nessie. The L.N.I.B. ended in 1972, but not before its many months of summer searching induced other scientific groups and individuals to take up the investigation.

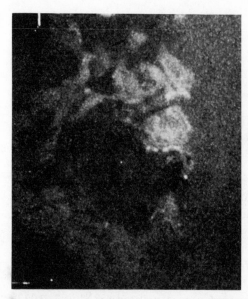

Since the first organized Loch Ness expedition in 1934, research groups have collected startling evidence on "Nessiteras rhombopteryx," like these underwater "head" and "body" photographs taken in the peat stained waters of Urquhart Bay in 1975 by the Academy of Applied Science. (courtesy: Academy of Applied Science)

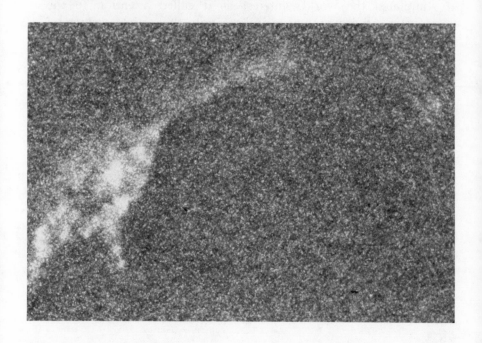

The most active group at Loch Ness during the 1970s was the American-based Academy of Applied Science. The A.A.S., using a high-technology approach to this mystery, has produced some excellent results utilizing sonar and subsurface photography. Their field work was so successful that, in 1975, Sir Peter Scott and Robert H. Rines dubbed Nessie with the scientific name "Nessiteras rhombopteryx"— the Ness monster with the diamond fin.

For fifty years various groups and dedicated individuals have seriously stalked these legendary Loch Ness beasties. They have employed a variety of methods and approaches in the quest, including: surface and subsurface photography, sonar, submarines, an autogyro, an airship, and there was even a proposed camera-equipped dolphin search of the loch. Although the evidence for Nessie's existence is weighty, the definitive proof still lies beyond the horizon, luring scientists and researchers from all over the world to the shores of Loch Ness. One day Lake Champlain may have that magnetic attraction in its scientific hunt for Champ.

The Search At Lake Champlain

ONE purpose of this book is to point out that Lake Champlain does indeed deserve a scientific search and study similar to that at Scotland's Loch Ness. No major institution or university has to date undertaken a long term, in depth cryptozoological investigation at Lake Champlain.

Yet Lake Champlain has received the cryptozoological acclaim to warrant such a study. Dr. Roy P. Mackal wrote in 1983, "Although there is a great deal of evidence for 'Lake Monsters' in lakes and rivers between 40° and 60° N. Latitude, other than Loch Ness, the best photographic evidence comes from Lake Champlain."

The Lake Champlain Phenomena Investigation was formed several years ago to meet this challenge and has conducted research, surface surveillance, sonar, and scuba monitoring at Lake Champlain. Hopefully, this privately financed investigation will act to persuade other persistent and dedicated individuals and

One of the most novel Champ searches was a 1978 six day wind-jammer expedition aboard the schooner Richard Robbins. Pictured here during that project is Canadian writer Dwight Whalen aboard the 80 foot sailing vessel. (photo credit: Joseph W. Zarzynski)

This Deep Sea MiniRover Mk II ROV (remotely-operated-vehicle) is a tethered underwater robot equipped with a video camera. The ROV was donated to the L.C.P.I.'s Champ field work in 1987 by Kaselaan & D'Angelo Associates, Inc. of Haddon Heights, New Jersey. The underwater robot is planned for future Champ-related expeditions and is ideal for surveying Lake Champlain's deep water which might hold a Champ carcass. (photo credit: M.P. Meaney)

organizations to devote their skills and time toward solving this North American enigma.

The first L.C.P.I. sponsored expedition was in 1980. It lasted several days and consisted of surface camera watches and sonar work at Button Bay, Vermont. Dwight Whalen, Don Fangboner, Paul and Bob Bartholomew, Richard Cowperthwait and myself participated in this expedition. Prior to that I had conducted numerous solo and small team field work sessions including an extended shore watching period with John Bierman during the summer of 1976 at Port Henry, New York, and a week-long 1978

Lake Champlain Phenomena Investigation associate, M.P. Meaney, is shown here camera watching at Loch Ness, Scotland in 1982. (photo credit: Joseph W. Zarzynski)

camera session from Panton, Vermont. In 1978 I coordinated a six day windjammer expedition in search of Champ aboard Dr. Kempton Webb's schooner RICHARD ROBBINS. 1979 saw Jim Kennard and myself in a side-scan sonar Champ expedition which included looking for a corporate jet which had crashed into Lake Champlain in the early 1970s.

The decade of the 1980s marked a more methodical approach to the Champ field work as I organized several field expeditions with a group of tireless individuals who became associates to the L.C.P.I.–M.P. Meaney, Jim Kennard, Scott Hill and Jack Sullivan. Blending the style of surface surveillance as that of the Loch Ness Investigation Bureau, and an underwater monitoring of select locations of Lake Champlain patterned after that practiced by the Academy of Applied Science at Loch Ness, the L.C.P.I. has averaged nearly one month of field work each year upon Lake Champlain from 1981–1987. This was accomplished, like many scientific excursions, on a shoestring budget, but with devoted personnel and the donation of much needed equipment.

The 1987 L.C.P.I. coordinated field work marked a significant upgrading of Champ searching equipment including the use of a Klein side-scan sonar, an underwater robot called a ROV, and experimentation with a video digitizer monitoring system for automated observation of the lake's surface. Gradually the scientific pursuit for Champ at Lake Champlain has taken a more sophisticated and systematic offensive to solving the Champ jigsaw puzzle.

CHAPTER 7

What Is Champ?

On the evidence that so far exists, most scientists decline to offer a working theory on Champ. However, according to Dr. Heuvelmans, the basic objective of cryptozoology is to accumulate available data on the "hidden" animal "so as to be able to put together a kind of identikit picture for it, to sketch the salient features of its behavior, to determine the nature of its habitat, the approximate limits of its area of distribution, and, eventually, to place it, with a reasonable degree of precision, in its proper zoological classification."[54]

Presently we can only contemplate the probable identity of Champ. Dr. Philip Reines, "a student of nautical phenomena since 1950,"[55] has proposed that a simple yardstick be employed to evaluate and gauge all reported Champ sightings. At the "Does Champ Exist?" Seminar held on August 29, 1981, in Shelburne, Vermont, Dr. Reines stated that all Champ sightings could be categorized into one of the following groupings: perpetrated hoax, honest misinterpretation, fantasy/illusion, reality.

Possibly one of the most difficult tests for a cryptozoologist is to weed out those recorded sightings which are cases of perpetrated hoax, honest misinterpretation or fantasy/illusion. Recently, too, critics and skeptics have been quick to point a finger of accusation stating that sightings of Champ are good for the tourist business. While this is probably true, the "Champ hoopla" is relatively minuscle compared to the volume of business already enjoyed by the tourist industry in and around the Lake Champlain basin.

Joseph W. Zarzynski (left) and Dr. Roy P. Mackal (center) during a news conference at the scientific conference, "Does Champ Exist?" Seminar, held in Shelburne, Vermont on August 29, 1981. (photo credit: M.P. Meaney)

I have hypothesized a list of what I believe people have observed in Lake Champlain and reported as Champ sightings. I have excluded the possibility that all Champ sightings are simply the product of perpetrated hoax. If this were true, several generations of very dedicated pranksters would have had to scheme in coordinated fashion and in great secrecy. Yes, the occasional hoax in the scientific world is a real possibility — one need only look at the Piltdown Man, the Cardiff Giant or New York's Lake George Monster Hoax of 1904–1906. In no manner of speaking, however, are all Champ sightings the result of deception.

Some reported Champ sightings may be explained as misinterpreting known phenomena. My list of possibilities of some of the "things" witnessed by observers and misconstrued as a legitimate Champ sighting includes:

1. Unique wave effect created by a passing surface vessel
2. Floating log(s) bobbing upon the lake's surface
3. Large sturgeon, gar pike or other fish
4. Atmospheric refraction — when surface temperature inversions produce optical trickery, thus causing known phenomena to become a "lake monster"
5. Swimming dog(s), floating bird(s), other known wildlife on the surface
6. Scuba diver(s)

My personal feeling is that the vast majority of reported sightings of Champ probably fall within the reality and honest misinterpretation categories.

The known evidence on Champ tends to imply that Champ is one of the following candidates:

- Amphibian — frogs, toads, salamanders
- Fish/eel — "supernormal" sturgeon, American eel
- Invertebrate — squids, worms, sea slugs
- Reptile — plesiosaur family
- Mammal — whales, seals, sea lions, dolphins

The amphibian, fish/eel and invertebrate groups each has some merit and following among researchers, but none of them entirely mesh with the collected data.

Most Champ students place the amphibian and invertebrate categories down the list of probable candidates. The fish/eel candidacy deserves special mention and discussion.

Lake sturgeon (Acipenser fulvescens Rafinesque) is a quite long lived fish that "is olive green on the back, gray on the sides, and light gray to white on the belly."[56] A bony fish, they prefer to stay near the bottom and are generally 5 to 6 feet long and average 30 to 40 pounds.[57] According to Charles W. Johnson, Vermont State Naturalist, the largest lake sturgeon caught in Vermont weighed just over 125 pounds. Lake sturgeon are rare and the taking of them from Lake Champlain is prohibited as they are an endan-

gered species. Some Champ sightings are probably attributable to
lake sturgeon, but it does not seem likely that Champ is an over-
grown lake sturgeon. And according to Daniel S. Plosila, an
aquatic biologist for the New York State Department of Environmental Conservation, ". . . it is unlikely that the Atlantic sturgeon
. . . enters Lake Champlain to spawn."[58]

As for the eel, according to William D. Countryman in *Checklist of the Recent Fishes of Vermont*, October, 1975, the family of
freshwater eel known to inhabit Lake Champlain is the "Anguilla
rostrata," or American eel, which averages three feet and has been
known to reach a length of 54 inches. Since this falls far short of
the dimensions reported in eyewitness sightings, I believe the
normal American eel may be dismissed as a likely candidate for
our Champ creature.

So we are left with the most enticing nominees, that Champ is
either a reptile or a mammal, possibly with prehistoric lineage.

*Some eyewitnesses of Champ may have observed known phenome-
na, such as a piece of driftwood, and misconstrued it as a sighting
of Champ. (photo credit: Joseph W. Zarzynski)*

In all probability some sightings of Champ may be of lake sturgeon. This 310 pound, 7 foot 6 inch long "monster" was taken from Lake Superior in 1922 and is considered by fishery experts to be one of the largest lake sturgeons on record. (credit: Ontario Department of Lands & Forests)

W.H. Lehn of the University of Manitoba's Department of Electrical Engineering suggests that some sightings of lake monster phenomena may be due to atmospheric image distortion. The first photograph shows a stick protruding from the ice in Lake Winnipeg. The other two photographs taken during conditions of surface temperature inversion show optical distortion. (© 1979 AAAS, courtesy: W.H. Lehn)

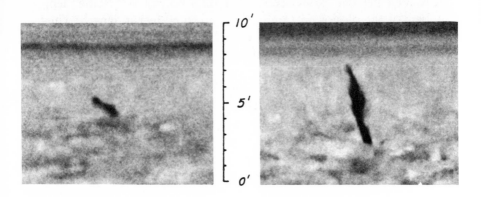

The American eel (Anguilla rostrata) is known to reach a length of about 54 inches. Thus, it is unlikely Champ is a member of this species. (courtesy: U.S. Fish and Wildlife Service)

Champ As A Plesiosaur

THE most often suggested aspirant for Champ from the prehistoric era is the marine reptile known as the plesiosaur, thought to have become extinct 60 to 70 million years ago.[59] Some members of the plesiosaur family grew up to 60 feet in length. They had a small head, long neck, wide body, long tail, and four flipper-like limbs used for propulsion.[60] Yet could these animals have survived? Is it possible that descendants of these prehistoric creatures — let's call them what they are: contemporaries of the dinosaur — are still around after 60 million years? Jules Verne-type visionaries would answer: Yes! Skeptics answer: No! Science has to say: We don't know, yet. Eyewitness reports and photographs indicate strong similarities in size and appearance, and the precedent has already been set by the coelacanth — thought extinct for approximately 70 million years — which has now been caught dozens of times off the Comoro Islands since being "rediscovered" in the late 1930s.

If we are to consider the plesiosaur as a candidate for Champ, we must assume they survived their presumed extinction — possibly through the sanctuary of the sea — and relocated from the oceans several thousand years ago to the now freshwater bodies of Lake Champlain and Loch Ness. We have already seen how this could have taken place in Lake Champlain, as its predecessor — the Champlain Sea — was an extension of the Atlantic Ocean. The question now, is, could plesiosaur Champ survive in the seasonal waters of Lake Champlain?

Plesiosaurs were reptiles, and the reptiles of our modern world are cold-blooded creatures. Cold-blooded animals derive their core body temperature from the environment in which they live, like fishes and amphibians. Warm-blooded animals have an internal ability for creating and keeping their core body temperatures independent of environmental temperatures, like birds and mammals. Today there is scientific speculation that some dinosaurs

Most Champ enthusiasts offer this marine reptile, the plesiosaur, as one of the most likely candidates for the "Lake Champlain Monster." The plesiosaur is believed to have become extinct approximately 60–70 million years ago. (credit: Bob Huntoon)

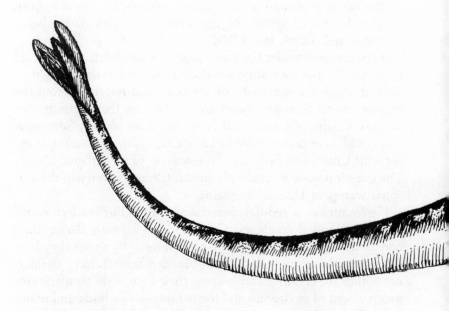

The zeuglodon, a snake-like primitive whale considered extinct for approximately 20 million years, is another nominee for Champ. (credit: Joseph MacDonough)

were warm-blooded, rather than the more orthodox theory of cold-blooded.

If Champ is found to be a plesiosaur, it may have adapted and developed slight warm-bloodedness to allow it to survive in Lake Champlain's cooler waters. In defense of this, Dr. Roy P. Mackal in his book, *The Monsters of Loch Ness*, writes: ". . . the Leatherback Turtle currently exhibits temperature adaptation significant enough to warrant our keeping an open mind on reptiles as a possible explanation for the Loch Ness phenomena."

Since plesiosaurs were air-breathers, plesiosaur Champ would appear to have to surface regularly. However, the adaptation of nostril-like "horns" that have been observed by some eyewitnesses on both Champ and Nessie suggest that these animals need just their snorkel-like horns to gather in air without showing more of

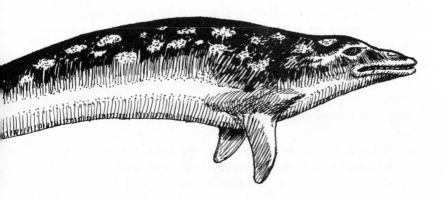

their massive bodies. Since Lake Champlain freezes over completely during most winters, if Champ were of a plesiosaur variety it may have developed some form of oxygen-retaining capabilities, thus allowing for longer periods of submergence. Or, like some reptiles, it may have developed a form of hibernation, such as certain aquatic turtles, which burrow into the mud under the waters to hibernate during the winter. Hence, it is conceivable that a colony of 15–25 foot long plesiosaur-like creatures could inhabit the vast depths of Lake Champlain. If it does turn out that Champ is a plesiosaur, it will be interesting to see how much they have evolved to permit them to reside in Lake Champlain's cooler environment.

Champ As A Zeuglodon

Mr. Gary S. Mangiacopra and Dr. Roy P. Mackal have hypothesized that Champ may be a mammal called a zeuglodon. These snake-like cetaceans, primitive whales, were thought to have

become extinct approximately 20 million years ago.[61] The zeuglodon, an ancestor of modern whales, had a single pair of front
limb flippers or appendages compared to the four flippers of the
plesiosaur. Zeuglodons, like plesiosaurs, were air breathers and
would have to surface on a regular basis to gather in life support-
ing air. As is true for most of our Champ candidates in account-
ing for the lake's annual freeze, the zeuglodons would either have
to be migratory or have developed a form of hibernation, or, as
Gary S. Mangiacopra has suggested, breathing holes could be
made by them, "in the manner that seals do in ice-locked regions,"
to remain in wintery Lake Champlain.

Another advocate of the zeuglodon hypothesis is Robert W.
Carroll, Jr., who has used his scientific background in cave investigation and related geological topics to study Lake Champlain's
"freeze over."

In 1984, Carroll wrote to me declaring that Champ "might be
able to maintain a series of isolated 'ice openings,' catch fish,
break thru refrozen spots, and even spasmodically sleep with
'nose out of the water'—and not have to migrate to the Gulf of St.
Lawrence each year. There is also a possibility they may have
some large lakeshore swamp with springs or even a cave to use
as a winter 'base of operations.' They could cover a few miles in
each underwater feeding foray. . . . It would be a precarious existence, but other creatures have done well on less. . . . These creatures could also use sonar and memory to relocate their base or
last 'air-hole'. . . ."

Carroll considers the zeuglodon hypothesis for Champ more
credible than the others. It's possible ". . . these creatures, like
muskrats, have dug tunnels into the extensive clay-bank shore-
lines—or widened naturally-occurring seepage 'clay-piping' tunnels—with offshore underwater exit and inland 'air pockets' that
stay above freezing. From there, they could either hibernate or
make under-the-ice feeding forays. But this is just speculation."

Champ As "Megalotaria longicollis"

ALTHOUGH most of the recent literature has indicated that the

Dr. Bernard Heuvelmans has hypothesized that Champ and other long-necked lake monsters are pinnipeds which he calls Megalotaria longicollis. (courtesy: Dr. Bernard Heuvelmans, redrawn by Rob DuBois)

Champ phenomenon may be a plesiosaur or zeuglodon, another candidate has recently been named. In January, 1983, Dr. Bernard Heuvelmans wrote to me suggesting that Champ is a pinniped—aquatic mammals including all the seals and walruses—with an elongated neck and from "its anatomy it seems to be closer allied to sea-lions than to seals."

Dr. Heuvelmans believes that the plesiosaur theory for Champ and other long-necked lake monsters is "purely romantic." He also declared the zeuglodon theory for Champ "is a little better, but does not hold."

"Just a look at the excellent Mansi's photograph shows very clearly that it cannot represent a plesiosaur," exclaimed Dr. Heuvelmans because of the neck structure in the Mansi photograph and the anatomy of the reptilian vertebrae.

Thus, Dr. Bernard Heuvelmans gives long-necked lake monsters, of which Champ is included, the provisional scientific name of "Megalotaria longicollis."

Champ As A Plesiosaur, A Zeuglodon, And A Seal-like Animal

I ₙ 1983, Mr. Gary S. Mangiacopra and Mr. John A. Heydt, in a letter sent to and published in the August, 1983 issue of *Champ Channels*, added another twist to the possible identity of Champ:

The current controversy to the zoological identification of Champ has produced several possible opinions from various cryptozoologists as to the candidates for its identification based upon the present data acquired . . . that Champ is a zeuglodon; a plesiosaur; and a seal-like animal. This possibility must be realized if indeed Lake Champlain is an "open lake" . . . . To which we answer we may be dealing with a situation of all three occurring simultaneously. . . . Thus, we must end with this question —"Champ, which one of the above are you or are you all three?"

The Champ Identikit

Sɪɴᴄᴇ one of the functions of a cryptozoologist is to project an identikit picture for the "hidden" animal, I would be remiss if I did not take that opportunity in the case of the Champ enigma. Below is a Champ identikit based on the more than two hundred known sightings of Champ.

ʙᴇʜᴀᴠɪᴏʀ: Shy; elusive; at times curious; passive; observed primarily during clear weather and a calm surface; observed mostly during the summer months [possibly due to more people on and near the lake or because the windless days present "con-

ditions during which fish, especially those of the salmon family
. . . rise to feed on insect hatches,"[62] thus giving Champ a possible food source (fish) near the surface].

SIZE: Their average calculated length is 26.25 feet.

COLOR: The most often reported colors are dark or black, gray,
brown.

SKIN: No general consensus on type of skin between smooth or
rough.

HEAD: Most often referred to as snake-like; also — round head,
horse's head, dinosaur head, dog's head, stove pipe head, peri-
scope head; two small horns atop head like ears; mouth with
teeth; two eyes; possible fringe on head; snout sometimes reported; approximately 37% of sightings observed head/neck.

HABITAT: Sightings scattered throughout all of Lake Champlain.

NUMBER: Believed to be more than one — 1983 included five sightings in which the eyewitnesses feel they saw more than one
Champ animal at the same time.

From this, a general composite can be hypothesized. Champ is
approximately 15–30 feet in length (taking into consideration that
the average reported length is 26.25 feet and that many estimates
of length tend to be overstated). It is dark or black in color with

*Mrs. Eva Gauvin and a friend saw Champ on August 27, 1983,
from Camp Marycrest, Grand Isle, Vermont, at a range of 300 yards.
(credit: Mrs. Eva Gauvin)*

some color differentiations possibly due to age or sex. Champ has a snake-like head with two horns or ears, a mouth and teeth, and a possible mane or fringe/ridge on its head and neck. Due to the infrequency of land sightings, there is no indication as to any or the number of flippers, but several eyewitnesses have observed a tail off the body. Champ has the ability to dive and swim at considerable speeds and can hold its head erect for a lengthy time. Weight is difficult to estimate, however, based on size descriptions, a body weight of several tons wouldn't be out of reason. A few eyewitnesses thought they may have heard a sound from the animal, but were not certain if this was due to surface splashing or voice/noise emission. Therefore, from the data we have, there is no definite consensus as to Champ's identity, except to declare that it is classified as an unidentified animal of large dimensions, and quite possibly is a breeding colony within Lake Champlain.

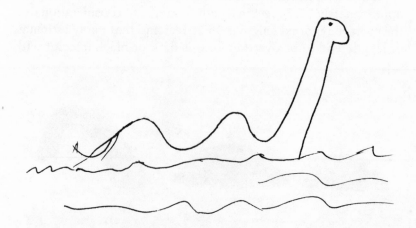

In 1976, Orville Wells saw Champ in Treadwell Bay, north of Platts-burgh, New York. This is his sketch of "a huge animal or whatever swimming very steadily and slowly across our bay . . . It appeared as something out of the past or [like a] prehistoric monster."
(credit: Orville Wells)

Dick L. and Timothy L. Noel saw Champ on June 14, 1983, off North Hero Island, Vermont, while eating their evening meal. They observed a dark 20–25 foot long creature, 3–4 feet high, at a range of 550 feet. (credit: Dick L. and Timothy L. Noel)

James A. and Gerda Carroll saw Champ on May 30, 1982, while on Lake Champlain in their yacht. "We saw a living creature swimming south [off Four Brothers Islands] on the surface of Lake Champlain. It was very large in comparison to the fish I am familiar with, both fresh and salt water, with the exception of whales, although without any of the mass of a whale." (credit: James A. and Gerda Carroll)

CHAPTER 8

Protection For Champ

With the fear that Champ might be hunted down and exterminated even prior to its formal acceptance as a species by science, the move for formal protection for Champ began in the late 1970s.

On December 21, 1977, the United States Department of the Interior published a news release entitled —"Are We Ready For 'Bigfoot' Or The Loch Ness Monster?" One of the aspects in this news release stated that if a Bigfoot-like or Loch Ness-type creature were suddenly and unequivocally proven to exist in the United States, "officials doubt whether any State or Federal action short of calling out the National Guard could keep order in the area within the first few hours or days of the creature's discovery." Therefore, it would seem wise to act prior to Champ's formal discovery and acceptance to establish protection to minimize aggressive action by humans against the Champ community.

Ground breaking for Champ's protection began on October 5, 1980. That evening I gave a lecture on Champ at the request of Mr. Greg Furness and Mr. Tim Titus at the Crown Point State Historic Site located across Bulwagga Bay from Port Henry, New York. One of the spectators in the audience, Mr. George Harrington, followed up on my plea calling for a lakeside town or village to pass a resolution protecting Champ. Mr. Harrington and other interested Village of Port Henry residents then convinced the Port Henry Village Board of Trustees to pass a resolution (October 6, 1980) declaring "that all the waters of Lake Champlain which

George Harrington (right) helped obtain the first Champ protection resolution passed by the Port Henry Village Board of Trustees and signed by Mayor Robert Brown (left). (photo credit: Warren F. Dobson, Warren Studio, Port Henry, NY)

ROBERT F. BROWN, MAYOR

Village of Port Henry

Port Henry, New York 12974

WHEREAS, the Lake Champlain Sea Monster, otherwise known as "Champ", has been inhabiting the waters of Lake Champlain for many years and,

WHEREAS, the existence of "Champ" has been documented by many of our North Country residents over the years, and

WHEREAS, "Champ" has recently attained international fame when the popular television program "Real People" interviewed many North Country residents concerning their personal observation concerning "Champ", and

WHEREAS, all endangered species are entitled to protection under both Federal and New York State laws, and

WHEREAS, "Champ" is apparently one of a kind, and hence its protection from harm, abuse and annihilation is vital,

NOW THEREFORE, BE IT RESOLVED BY THE VILLAGE BOARD OF THE VILLAGE OF PORT HENRY that all the waters of Lake Champlain which adjoin the Village of Port Henry are hereby declared to be off limits to anyone who would in any way harm, harass or destroy the Lake Champlain Sea Monster.

ADOPTED BY THE PORT HENRY VILLAGE BOARD OF TRUSTEES ON OCTOBER 6, 1980.

adjoin the Village of Port Henry are hereby declared to be off limits to anyone who would in any way harm, harass or destroy the Lake Champlain Sea Monster."

Armed with this precedent, Vermont House Representative Millie Small of Quechee, Vermont, expressed an interest in having the Vermont House of Representatives pass a resolution protecting Champ.

A public hearing sponsored by the Vermont House Natural Resources Committee was convened in Montpelier, Vermont, the

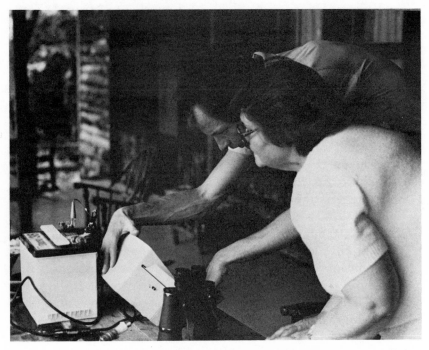

Mr. Joseph W. Zarzynski with Vermont House Representative Millie Small during her visit to the Lake Champlain Phenomena Investigation field camp at Lake Champlain in 1981. Rep. Small introduced a resolution to the Vermont House protecting Champ and encouraging further scientific inquiry into the phenomenon. The resolution was passed by the Vermont House on April 20, 1982. (photo credit: M.P. Meaney)

evening of February 26, 1981, on the "Lake Champlain Monster." Rep. Small and I had hoped this hearing would generate enough response in this legislative body that she could introduce the resolution to the Vermont House of Representatives during the 1981 legislative session. Although the public hearing was greeted with positive public support, the Champ resolution had to wait until 1982. Rep. Small felt that there was not enough favorable political sentiment in 1981 to introduce the resolution.

Finally, the Champ resolution, entitled H.R. 19, was passed by the Vermont House on April 20, 1982, by a 77 to 28 vote.[63] This resolution, which I drafted in late 1980 with the advice of Mayor Erastus Corning II of Albany, Mr. Dean Coon (attorney), Mr. Monty Fischer (director of the Lake Champlain Basin Program), Mr. Robert Hohmann and Mr. John Ray, was introduced to the Vermont House by Rep. Millie Small. Her courage and determination in getting this resolution passed must not be minimized.

An event that no doubt accorded this resolution impetus and momentum was the August 29, 1981 "Does Champ Exist?" Seminar. The major sponsor for this seminar, held at the handsome and rustic Coach Barn, Shelburne Farms estate, Shelburne, Vermont, was the Lake Champlain Committee. This organization, as already mentioned, is a 1,500 member strong environmental watchdog for Lake Champlain. On the program were: Dr. William H. Eddy, Jr., University of Vermont and President of Environmental Concerns International, Inc.; Sandra Mansi; Mr. J. Richard Greenwell of the University of Arizona; Dr. George Zug, Chairman, Department of Vertebrate Zoology at the National Museum of Natural History, Smithsonian Institution, Washington, D.C.; Dr. Roy P. Mackal, Department of Biology, University of Chicago; Dr. Philip Reines, Department of Communications, S.U.N.Y. at Plattsburgh; and myself. The L.C.P.I. was also one of the financial sponsors of this seminar. This scientific seminar was attended by approximately 200 people from all corners of life. The seminar did much to help educate the public, the scientific community and the media on the Champ phenome-

New York State Senator Ronald B. Stafford sponsored the Champ resolution passed by the New York State Senate on June 3, 1982. (courtesy: Ronald B. Stafford)

STATE OF NEW YORK
—•—
The Legislature
ALBANY

LEGISLATIVE RESOLUTION
Assembly No. 112

IN ASSEMBLY
By Members of Assembly A.W. Ryan, Harris, Casale, Conners and McCann:

> Legislative resolution encouraging serious scientific inquiry into the existence of unusual animals in Lake Champlain, especially one commonly known as "Champ"; protecting Champ from any willful act resulting in death, injury or harassment; and encouraging report of sighting of such animals

Whereas, There are documented reports, historical accounts, and photographic evidence to substantiate the possible existence in Lake Champlain of an unidentified aquatic animal or animals described as long-necked, serpentine, or snakelike; and

Whereas, The animals of this kind have been part of the Champlain Valley folklore for over three and a half centuries, to the enjoyment of all citizens of the state; and

Whereas, These animals have been observed by many citizens of the state and others; and

Whereas, The discovery of a species of heretofore unknown animal life would be a contribution to the fund of human knowledge; and

as, Recent publicity has generated considerable scientific curiosity to investigate these animals; and

Whereas, The absence of a state law to protect these unidentified unknown animals may encourage the use of force or violence, threatening their welfare and the safety of New Yorkers and people enjoying the beauty of Lake Champlain; and

The "Champ Resolution" passed by the New York State Assembly on

Protection for Champ

—2—

Whereas, No act of violence by these animals has every been recorded against any individual or group of people; and

Whereas, The most responsible course for the state of New York to follow would be to encourage continued collection and evaluation of scientific evidence of unexplained phenomena in Lake Champlain; now, therefore, be it

Resolved, That the possible existence of the animal commonly known as "Champ" is recognized by this state; and be it further

Resolved, That "Champ" should be protected from any willful act resulting in death, injury or harassment; and be it further

Resolved, That the State of New York encourage serious scientific inquiry into the existence of any unusual animals in Lake Champlain, especially the possible existence of an animal such as the one commonly known as "Champ"; and be it further

Resolved, That citizens of New York and visitors to Lake Champlain are encouraged to report sightings of such animals or associated phenomena and photographic evidence whenever possible.

By order of the Assembly,

Catherine A. Carey
Catherine A. Carey, Clerk

ADOPTED IN ASSEMBLY ON
April 18, 1983

April 18, 1983. (courtesy: New York State Assembly)

non, and was probably the single most motivating event toward passage of state resolutions on Champ.

The Champ resolution has also been passed by the New York State Senate, on June 3, 1982, with sponsorship by State Senator Ronald B. Stafford. On April 18, 1983, the New York State Assembly passed the Champ resolution sponsored by Assemblymen Ryan, Harris, Casale, Conners and McCann. Finally, on April 29, 1986, the Vermont Senate adopted the Champ resolution.

These state resolutions protect Champ, promote serious scientific inquiry into the Champ phenomenon and encourage individuals to report sightings.

In a letter to me of April 26, 1983, New York State Assemblyman Anthony J. Casale called the Champ resolution a "guiding light for serious scientific inquiry."

Paleontologists have estimated that today's animals represent only approximately 2 percent of the estimated half-billion species believed to have existed during Planet Earth's history.[64] Mayor Erastus Corning II of Albany, New York, now deceased, summed up the spirit of the Champ protection movement in a letter to me dated December 29, 1980:

In the past we have destroyed much of what we have found. The monster can be a very large and exciting symbol of the fact that we should not destroy what is on the earth, but live in harmony with it.

Hopefully in Quebec, Canada, authorities will adopt legal protection for Champ as five miles of the 109 mile long Lake Champlain does reside in Quebec.

CHAPTER 9

How To Prove Champ's Existence

THE question remains . . . what is required to prove Champ's existence?

To some people the evidence already accumulated is enough. A statement made by Mr. G.K. Chesterton about Loch Ness indeed applies to Lake Champlain: "Many a man has been hanged on less evidence than there is for the Loch Ness Monster."[65]

However, other people demand undisputed, definitive photographs or film footage of one of the animals as satisfactory evidence for Champ's existence. And there would still be others who would only believe in Champ if a piece of its tissue were secured or a bone from a carcass acquired.

Dr. Roy P. Mackal believes that Champ photographic evidence will never settle the issue. "A specimen, preferably a live one, will be required for that. Then and only then will we be able to arrive at a final classification of these creatures."[66]

Dr. C.L. Smith, one of the most respected scientists in the world and a member of the Department of Ichthyology at New York City's American Museum of Natural History, recently wrote on his philosophy about Champ:

. . . once a specimen is found, Champ will no longer belong to cryptozoology. Then it will fall within the purview of zoologists, like me, who study known organisms. We can investigate its structure, its physiology, behavior, life span, etc. We will try to devise methods of ensuring its continuing survival and we will work out its relationships to other known organisms, living and fossil. With a specimen in hand, Champ will be just one more rare species.[67]

Thus it would appear the scientific community needs, or at least prefers, a physical specimen of Champ — dead or alive. Although I once contemplated a netting operation to secure a creature for temporary, controlled study, I now have come to support a more passive approach. I personally feel we need to gather more sighting information, sonar and photographic evidence. Possibly a meticulous bottom search of Lake Champlain for a carcass would prove rewarding. Further investigative work under controlled conditions in cooperation with state and federal agencies, might lead to carefully isolating one of the Champ animals in a bay, to be photographed and safely released. Until we know more about these magnificent animals, a netting operation could harm one of them and thus be detrimental to the survival and breeding of the existing colony.

So the relentless search at North America's Loch Ness, its documentation and protective legislation lobbying must not falter. For those who would label this investigation a scientific folly, Dr. C.L. Smith has a timely reply:

What if there is no Champ? Supposing it suddenly became possible to explore the entire lake and all of its underwater hiding places simultaneously so that there could be no doubt that Champ does not exist. Would that mean that all of the efforts of those who have searched in vain were wasted? I don't think so. It seems to me that we are all a little richer because of the dedicated people who have had the curiosity to look for something that may or may not exist. Curiosity is a human trait and the unabashed curiosity of those who seek Champ adds to the humanity of all mankind. May the search never cease![68]

Aye, may that much treasured and elusive answer await those who persevere in their quest for scientific knowledge and the exploration for CHAMP — BEYOND THE LEGEND!

And The Search Goes On

The fascinating history of the search for Nessie has produced a fine museum at Loch Ness devoted entirely to "Nessiteras rhombopteryx." Hopefully the search at Lake Champlain will generate enough interest to develop a Champ museum/visitors center along the shores of Lake Champlain. (photo credit: Joseph W. Zarzynski)

"Does Champ Exist?—
A Scientific Seminar"

On Saturday, August 29, 1981 a scientific seminar on the Champ phenomenon was held at The Coach Barn, Shelburne Farms, Shelburne, Vermont.

This Seminar was unique to North America in that it was the first of its kind on Champ. It compares in magnitude, scientific interest, and in the quality of its speakers to the meeting convened on December 10, 1975 in the Grand Committee Room of Parliament in London, United Kingdom to discuss Nessie, the Loch Ness phenomenon. That London meeting was prompted by a series of underwater photographs taken in June, 1975 by the American-based Academy of Applied Science of an unidentified animate object in the peat stained depths of Loch Ness. Two hundred people including members of Parliament, British and American scientists, media correspondents, and other guests listened to testimony on Nessie's existence. That scientific gathering was later described by Loch Ness researcher and author, Nick Witchell, in his book, THE LOCH NESS STORY, as "Nessie's 'finest hour.' "

In a similar atmosphere, too, was the "Does Champ Exist?" Seminar greeted by all its participants and observers.

The "Does Champ Exist?" Seminar was primarily the child of the Lake Champlain Committee and Vermont State Representative Millie Small of Quechee, Vermont. It was initiated by a desire to discuss in a serious and open manner the evidence on the Champ phenomenon.

The Seminar's financial sponsors were: the Lake Champlain Committee, the Lake Champlain Basin Program — NERBC, Joseph W. Zarzynski — L.C.P.I., The Environmental Program — University of Vermont, the Plattsburgh & Clinton County, New York Chamber of Commerce, Shelburne Farms, R. and E. Sincerbeaux of Woodstock, Vermont, and the Port Henry, New York Chamber of Commerce.

The scheduled participating speakers included: Dr. William H. Eddy, Jr. (Adjunct Assistant Professor, The Environmental Program — University of Vermont, and President, Environmental Concerns International, Inc.) who acted as Seminar moderator; Joseph W. Zarzynski (Founder and Director of The Lake Champlain Phenomena Investigation) who lectured with the aid of slides and an overhead projector on the "Historical Background" on Champ; Sandra Mansi and other eyewitnesses of Champ; Dr. Philip Reines (Department of Mass Communication, State University of New York, Plattsburgh) who lectured and played audio tapes on the subject of "Analysis of Phenomena Sightings"; J. Richard Greenwell (Secretary, Arid Lands Natural Resources Committee, University of Arizona, Tucson, and cofounder of The International Society of Cryptozoology) who lectured with the aid of slides on "Does Champ Exist? — Current Scientific Evidence"; Dr. George Zug (Chairman, Department of Vertebrate Zoology, National Museum of Natural History, Smithsonian Institution, Washington, D.C.) who presented a talk entitled "Champ: fact or fiction, illusion or imagination?" during the segment on "Does Champ Exist? — Current Scientific Evidence"; and Dr. Roy P. Mackal (Department of Biology, University of Chicago, and cofounder of The International Society of Cryptozoology) who lectured with the aid of slides on "Does Champ Exist? — Current Scientific Evidence."

This appendix is a selected excerpt kindly provided by the Lake Champlain Committee. The manuscript was transcribed and written by Eloise Hedbor and edited for inclusion for this appendix by Joseph W. Zarzynski and Robert DuBois.

When the Lake Champlain Committee decided to sponsor a

scientific seminar, "Does Champ Exist?", we did not expect to get a definitive, indisputable and conclusive answer.

We take no official position on the matter ourselves, though, it must be admitted, some of us individually hold strong and diverse opinions on the subject.

But, if there is some sort of strange and, most probably, rare creature dwelling in the depths of Lake Champlain, it has a right to continue living there. And people have an obligation to protect it, from direct harm and from degredation of its environment.

So, does Champ exist? Can Champ exist? And what, if anything, should we do about this possibility?

"DOES CHAMP EXIST?" SEMINAR

Introduction: Introductory Remarks By Dr. William H. Eddy, Jr. (Seminar Moderator)

Historical Background: Joseph W. Zarzynski

There have been scattered reports of "something" in Lake Champlain for many years, but no organized serious effort to determine just what people were seeing, until 1974.

Joseph W. Zarzynski, a Social Studies teacher in Saratoga Springs, New York, is the founder of the Lake Champlain Phenomena Investigation. Since 1974 he has collected and correlated information on Champ and other aquatic creatures that may be "cousins." In addition to Nessie, there are reports of unexplained large aquatic animals in Iceland, Scandinavia, British Columbia, and other lands.

Although he has yet to personally sight "Champ," Zarzynski is convinced there is not one but a small breeding community of "Champ" animals somewhere in the depths of Lake Champlain.

During his lecture at the Seminar he compared Lake Champlain to Loch Ness — their physical similarities and their history of sightings of unidentified animals.

Since he began his investigations in 1974, Zarzynski has catalogued over 200 possible sightings of Champ (144 catalogued sightings reported at the August 29, 1981 Seminar). Some, he admits, may be sturgeon or other large fish, logs or something else explainable. "Some, however, you simply cannot dismiss," he declares. Approximately 40% of these sightings involve a head and neck stretching out of the water.

As Zarzynski and others have begun to look at the Lake Champlain Monster seriously, the number of reported sightings has increased steadily. Zarzynski believes this is attributable to several factors. The greater numbers of people on the lake in recent years has increased the opportunities for sightings, he says. He also postulates that over the years Champs (or the families of Champs) have become acclimated to the boat traffic and less frightened by it. Furthermore, serious investigation has created a more positive atmosphere, and those who report sightings are less likely to be ridiculed for coming forward with their experience.

Zarzynski reported at the Seminar that the greatest number of sightings occur in July and August, which also happen to be the months when the greatest number of people are on the lake or its shores. Sightings have been reported in many places up and down the lake, at all different times of the day and even at night. These reports, although not providing conclusive scientific evidence, offer tantalizing clues.

EYEWITNESSES — ACCOUNTS OF THEIR SIGHTINGS
Sandra Mansi:

Sandra Mansi is not a person who will speculate about whether Champ exists. She knows it exists, she says, having "met" and photographed an apparently furtive animal on July 5, 1977.

Scientists have verified that the 1977 Mansi photo is not a composite, but they have not been able to say definitely what it is. Mrs. Mansi does not have the negative which would allow computer enhancement and enlargement of the picture to obtain greater detail. And she cannot say just where the picture was taken, just somewhere near St. Albans, Vermont.

Meanwhile, Mrs. Mansi says now her greatest fear is "that I

have opened a Pandora's Box." She says she worries now about Champ and about people who live on the lake — swimmers and divers, and people who enjoy the tranquility of Lake Champlain.

"We've got to do something to protect it," says Mrs. Mansi. "This creature is so magnificent and so wonderful that it has learned to co-exist with us. Now let us learn to co-exist with it." [For more information on Sandra and Anthony Mansi's photograph, consult the text.]

Mary Carty:

Mary Carty, a native Vermonter, describes herself as a "budding photographer," which, she says, is why she happened to have a camera with her on July 17, 1981.

While driving along, approaching the Shelburne Farms estate, someone "suddenly came running up from the beach, yelling, 'It's Champ! It's Champ,'" said Ms. Carty.

"Now I didn't believe him at first but he looked really serious. . . . So I reached in the back seat and I got the camera out. By the time I got down to the beach, the creature had gone back underwater. (The other people on the beach) had seen a neck come out and it just sat there."

"I started taking pictures. The creature was moving from south to north and it kept moving and there were more humps. At one time there were six humps out of the water."

Ms. Carty claimed to have taken "a sequence of about 17 pictures."

She estimated that what she and the other people saw on the beach that day was probably 30 feet long from head to tail.

"It may have been some kind of sturgeon. I don't know. But it is very large, and I'm thinking it's something like a serpent, a snake-like creature," said Ms. Carty.

Eugene Viens, Jr.:

Eugene Viens, Jr., also a native Vermonter, first became interested in Champ more than a decade ago.

"One time I was on the Lookout Rock. . .off from North Beach.

You can see over the harbor here in Burlington. We were up there with two other people and. . .we noticed (what) appears to be the same wake that would be formed by a boat, but no boat. At that time I saw these high spots. . .four high spots, one that would appear to be the head. It was quite large. I would estimate about 30 feet long. . .I do think it moved between seven and 10 miles an hour. It traveled at a pretty good pace. It seemed to swim rather straight, not very much movement but a huge wake."

Elsie Porter: (taken from a tape recording played by Dr. Reines at the Seminar during his speaking session)

Elsie Porter, 61, is a resident of the New York side of the lake, and reports not a single, but multiple sightings of Champ many years ago. When she was a young girl her family owned some land "up on the bluff about two miles north of the ferry dock on the New York side."

She and her brother "used to sit on the white bench up on the bluff waiting for the trains to come so we could wave to the conductors."

Elsie Porter said that "many times we saw something that came out of the water this side of the Port Kent Ferry in deep water but about halfway from the bluff to the ferry. . .It quietly came up and I think we saw it for years and years, but we assumed everyone else knew it was there. . .

"I never saw any horns on it. . .it had a long neck that looked like a snake to me, and either some bumps on his back or fins or something. . .

". . .I would say it was as big as a rhinoceros' back when it came up. I mean the same texture only grey—black or brown—dark whatever it was. It could have been dark green. . .

"It didn't just submerge. The head went right out straight and went down. . .it extended its neck and then went down. . .

"It made no noise coming up and it didn't make any noise that I could hear going down and it was just peaceful like the day," recalls Mrs. Porter. She and her brother were "never frightened" by the creature.

She described a typical sighting in this way. "I saw the head come up first and then the back. . .It seemed it had three humps, like a camel, only more pointed — they were separate. . .The head was more like an anaconda, a boa constrictor kind of head, a thick strong head. . .We saw it so many times. . ."

Joan Petro:

Joan Petro, a freelance journalist and a Port Henry, New York publicity person who has written about Champ, herself, saw this mysterious creature a few years ago. She also reported a sighting August 28, 1981, by a group of 17 Bible school children who said they saw Champ in the lake off the hill in Port Henry by the Catholic Church.

LUNCH AND NEWS CONFERENCE

Analysis of Phenomena Sightings — Dr. Philip Reines

Dr. Philip Reines, professor of mass communications at the State University of New York at Plattsburgh, has had a long-time interest in Champ, but he continues to take the role of a devil's advocate in the search for the truth about Champ — like sightings.

"I do believe in the existence of officially hitherto unidentified animals, wonderful animals," Reines acknowledges. "I have always been a follower of mysteries of the sea."

Nevertheless, he insists, it is imperative that serious investigators maintain a strict objectivity, suspend all personal opinion, and instead apply the most stringent yardstick to measure the veracity of each report, each piece of evidence.

Champ may be an oversized specimen of a known animal, says Reines. There are scattered, and of course, unconfirmed, reports of huge sturgeon in Lake Champlain, far exceeding the ordinary five or eight-foot specimen. That fish, rolling on the surface, would present an astonishing sight, and would, inself, be a major discovery.

Likewise, says Reines, are unconfirmed stories of gigantic eels, far larger than the five foot length that is normal for the American eel.

On the Mansi photo, Dr. Reines asks — was the Mansi picture actually taken on Lake Champlain? If so, what sort of place is it? Shallow or deep? Sheltered or exposed? So far, efforts to find the site have proved fruitless.

If the location of the picture can be found and if it is on Lake Champlain, "it will give clues" about Champ, says Reines.

DOES CHAMP EXIST? — CURRENT SCIENTIFIC EVIDENCE

J. Richard Greenwell:

J. Richard Greenwell reports that detailed analysis by experts reveals of the Mansi photograph that there are "definitely no cuts, no superimposition," but, he warns, that "does not mean it is a monster or a living object. It does mean an object was there and was photographed."

A careful analysis of the wave patterns, Greenwell reports, seems to indicate that the disturbance in the water surrounding the unidentified object was caused by that object.

Computer enhancements of the color print have yielded more intriguing hints, but little definitive information. One of the most serious problems with using the Mansi photo as evidence, says Greenwell, is that the negative is missing. It is possible enlargements from such a negative would give much greater detail and provide answers to many questions.

In another analysis, Greenwell compared the Mansi photo with one taken at Loch Ness a number of years ago by a London surgeon, Dr. Wilson. Although the position of the subject differed as did the camera angle, the two photos appear to show similar objects.

Tracings revealed a high degree of correlation between the two photos, and the objects captured on film appear to be "practically identical in size," says Greenwell.

"The whole head and neck posture is very similar (which could) lead one to speculate (it is) the same or similar species," he says.

Dr. George Zug:

Champ: fact or fiction, illusion or imagination?

The other speakers are addressing this question directly. My approach is more circuitous and, in fact, is concerned with the phenomenon in general and not the sightings at Lake Champlain in particular.

I wish to examine a single basic issue in the search for unknown animals or mysterious monsters, whether they be Champ, Nessie, Ogopogo or Chessie.

What is the possibility of the existence of a population of large (10 ft or longer) aquatic animals in close proximity to man and yet remaining largely unknown and unseen?

I cannot offer a solution to such a possibility in terms of statistical probability.

However, what I can offer are some examples from recent biological discoveries that relate to the Champ phenomenon.

Perhaps the best way to begin is with discoveries about a well known animal's biology, and not the discovery of a new species.

The importance of the following example is to demonstrate that what we know and then what we assume from this knowledge makes us blind to opposing observations or prone to misinterpret reliable — although strange — observations.

My example involves large marine turtles in the waters off the coast of New England, Nova Scotia and Newfoundland.

The marine turtles of concern to us are the leatherbacks. Leatherbacks are the largest living turtles. Shell lengths of adults range from four to six feet long and adults weigh from 600 to 1000 lbs. The turtles are jet black with widely scattered white flecking. The shell above and below bears a series of longitudinal ridges and is covered by a leathery skin — hence their name. In many features, they are highly peculiar turtles and potential myth-makers; however we are discovering that their actual lives are stranger than fiction.

For decades, leatherback sea turtles have been observed regularly, although infrequently, in the cold waters of the northwest

Atlantic. These turtles nest on the tropical beaches of Central and South America, so obviously the leatherbacks in the north Atlantic were waifs — strays doomed to drift further north and die from exposure to cold and starvation. That was our assumption and was widely and dogmatically accepted until this past decade when our acceptance of the validity of this interpretation was undermined.

The erosion of the old doctrine probably dates to 1965 when a Canadian biologist reported that, according to local fishermen, the occurrence of leatherbacks in Nova Scotia waters was an annual event.

He further examined the stomach contents of some leatherbacks drowned in the fishermen's nets.

Surprisingly the stomach contents were jelly fish — an unlikely natural prey for a giant turtle.

Subsequent analyses continue to support jelly fish as the predominant food of leatherbacks.

The next step in the change of our view was a survey of sea turtle sightings and strandings in Europe. Leatherback occurrences were much commoner than previously supposed, and this commonness was being confirmed by a more regular and systematic compilation of sightings along the North American coast.

In the early seventies, it was reported that leatherbacks appeared to regularly maintain their body temperatures above that of the surrounding water. And shortly thereafter anatomical dissections demonstrated that leatherbacks had a countercurrent arrangement of arteries and veins in their limbs which effectively reduced heat loss in cold waters.

In the mid and late seventies, scientists from the University of Rhode Island began to make regular aerial surveys to document whale migration and diversity off the coast of New England. They soon discovered that whales were not the only animals migrating along the coast, but leatherbacks were regular migrants also — heading north in the spring and south in the late summer.

Our view of leatherbacks has changed drastically — from cold-blooded animals lost and dying in the cold North Atlantic to warmblooded animals, migrating annually to northern waters to eat jellyfish.

Now what is the point of this discourse on leatherback sea turtles? No, I am definitely not suggesting that the objects called Champ are leatherbacks.

What I wish to illustrate is that if 15, perhaps even 10 years ago, lay observers had reported flotillas of large black animals with hump backs and pig-like heads passing off the coast of Maine, they would have been considered as liars, drunks, imagining things, or misreporting a school of fish or a pod of whales.

When, in fact, they were accurately reporting their observations.

Clearly our knowledge — perhaps even our faith — in an event changes our perception of the event.

How we see and interpret the Champ phenomenon today will undoubtedly be altered by our persistent re-analysis of the Champ observations and further changed by the accumulation of harder, more technical, data.

The leatherback example makes two points in this regard: (1) Don't discount a known species of animals from possessing unknown and unanticipated behaviours or traits. (2) Biological events must be viewed in an open-minded manner for the unexpected is not necessarily improbable.

Another aspect of the presence of large, but rarely seen animals living in close proximity to man is the absence of carcasses washing ashore.

Obviously a carcass washing ashore would resolve the mystery.

Why haven't we discovered such carcasses? The absence of such strandings leads the skeptics to deny the existence of the Champ phenomenon as a natural event or at least to reject the phenomenon as resulting from a large aquatic animal.

Two points are relevant here: (1) Negative evidence can neither validate or invalidate an observation, hence serves no useful function in our examination of the Champ phenomenon. (2) Strandings of carcasses are not common phenomena! Not common in the sense of the proportion of animals washing ashore relative to the numbers dying.

Allow me to give two examples which bear on uncommonness of strandings.

First, another sea turtle example.

The loggerhead sea turtles in the southeastern United States suffer high mortality owing to their propensity to be caught and drawn in shrimp trawls.

Preliminary experiments have been performed to determine the proportion of dead turtles washing ashore. The results were variable, ranging from none in one test to 40% in another test. At best, we can estimate that one out of every three or four turtles drowned will wash ashore.

So when we have a season with hundreds washing ashore, we can assume thousands died.

Perhaps a better example is the stranding of beaked whales, because here we are dealing with natural deaths and not man-accelerated death rates.

At the Smithsonian, our Marine Mammal Program maintains records on the strandings of all cetaceans. This is possible because of a network of active coast watchers – amateurs and professionals alike – who regularly report their observations thru a Scientific Events Alert Network and allow our marine mammalogist to accurately record the occurrence and frequency of whale strandings.

Species of high abundance and living in shallow coastal waters, such as bottlenose dolphins, show a high stranding rate with hundreds washing ashore each year, predominantly in the winter months. The stranding of these dolphins is sufficiently common, and with representatives of all age classes, that our marine mammalogist is able to reconstruct the demography and reproductive cycles of local populations.

The frequent stranding of these dolphins and a few similar species is more the exception than the rule.

Most whale species strand much less frequently. The beaked whales clearly illustrate the rarity of stranding. There are six species of beaked whales in the North Atlantic. All look like giant bottlenose dolphins with their bulbous foreheads and elongated beaks, but they range in length from 14 to 35 feet. They are largely pelagic animals, living in the open ocean, and are relatively solitary. These habits result in fewer strandings.

The Cuvier's beaked whales (Ziphius cavirostris) are by far the most common members of the beaked whale family and occur in all the world's oceans. Our records show that a total of 330 strandings have been reported since 1804 — of these 40 occurred on the Atlantic coast of North America. This averages out to one stranding every four years on our coastline. A closer examination of the records reveals that the strandings were roughly one per decade until the 1950s when reports of marine mammals became more systematic.

In the seventies, with the establishment of the marine mammal salvage network, a total of nine strandings were reported. This is only one stranding per year for over 3000 miles of coastline. Hardly a common event considering the length of the coastline and the organized reporting network.

Yet in contrast to the other beaked whale species, it is a species which strands commonly.

For example, Blainville's beaked whale (Mesoplodon densirostris) is also a species with a worldwide distribution. But only 31 individuals have been reported since 1839, and only 15 of these from our Atlantic seaboard.

True's beaked whale (Mesopoldon mirus) is a species restricted to the North Atlantic. Only 18 have been reported since 1899, 12 from the North American coast.

How do these examples relate to the Champ phenomenon, assuming it is produced by a population of large aquatic animals?

First, the possibility of a carcass washing ashore would be a rare event. Using the turtle data, the laws of change, at best, predict one out of three dead or dying animals washing ashore. The probability of stranding would be further decreased by the rarity of the animals and a likely lower death rate. If, like dolphins, most deaths occur in the winter, the probability of a carcass washing ashore becomes infinitesimal.

Even if a carcass floats ashore, the likelihood of its discovery is low. There is no regular patrol of the lake's shores as exist for the marine mammal salvage network, and the shores don't have wide sandy beaches to toss a carcass on nor regular tidal surges to leave the carcass high and dry.

A stranding may be hoped for, but not counted on, to solve the mystery.

Certainly the absence of a stranded carcass does not negate the possible existence of large aquatic animals; however the absence does not support the existence of such creatures either.

In conclusion, the purpose of my examples drawn from relatively well known animals is to demonstrate that the search for verification of Champ as a population of large aquatic animals is not an easy task nor one that is likely yield instantaneous results.

The difficulties do not negate the desirability or the need for a search for reliable and accurate data. The difficulties do call, however, for encouragement and tolerance of those individuals who honestly and critically investigate the Champ phenomenon.

Dr. Roy P. Mackal:

Using the many monster sightings in Lake Champlain, Loch Ness and elsewhere, Dr. Mackal has attempted to find clues to how these hypothetical creatures live.

As Greenwell explained, monsters have been primarily reported only in bodies of water that retain a link to the sea, where salmon, eels or other fish are known to return from the ocean for spawning.

Mackal suggests these animals, normally denizens of the open ocean, occasionally or maybe periodically venture into fresh water lakes possibly in pursuit of food such as salmon. Creatures similar to the lake monsters have been reported along the coastal regions of North America and northern Europe.

The apparent habits and general descriptions given by observers seem to Dr. Mackal to indicate these monsters are a mammal fully adapted to aquatic life, possessing front flippers, and capable of diving to considerable depths. But the consistantly reported elongated shape fits no known living aquatic mammal.

Mackal, however, does see a number of similarities between the descriptions and a primitive elongated whale, the zeuglodon. (Greenwell offered the hypothesis that Champ may be a type of marine reptile, the long-thought extinct plesiosaur).

The zeuglodon is not a perfect match for Champ and his cousins. It possessed only a short neck and thus could not rear out of the water as the elusive monsters apparently do. But, perhaps Champ is a relative of the zeuglodon, which developed a long neck in response to some evolutionary demands.

Mackals' hypothesis is not, of course, universally accepted. Yet, whatever this creature might be, it is wide spread, relatively rare, extremely surreptitious in its behavior, and probably a denizen of the deep where, in death, its body remains, far from curious scientists' eyes.

Mackal also adds one more piece of puzzling evidence. The creature is not limited to any single body of water or waterway system. Its survival in fact suggests an animal able to migrate from one body of water to another, possibly stimulated by dwindling food supplies or severe seasons, any sort of inhospitable change. He says there are rare but persistent reports that these animals are able to move out on land at least to an extent! According to Dr. Mackal the final answer will not come until an actual specimen can be examined.

Interim Report/
Lake Champlain 'Monster' Photograph

DR. B. ROY FRIEDEN
Optical Sciences Center
University of Arizona

(April 30, 1981)

From what I can see, the photo does not appear to be a montage or a superposition of any kind. The object appears to belong in the picture, and I say that because there seems to be a separate set of surface waves coming from it that are independent from the waves of the rest of the lake. That would make it much more difficult a hoax by superposition—you would have had to hoax a separate set of waves as well and that gets to be too difficult a problem.

Also, we don't see any evidence of tampering with the photo, that is, any sharp demarcation lines indicating a superposition. We have not yet confirmed distance and size. This seems to be possible with trigonometric calculation, although you'd have to know the approximate height above the lake to really know the distance out. But that could be estimated, I suppose.

Generally, the photo is a very sharp, crisp photo and what we suspected was that the colors would be saturated—and all the densities saturated—all the way as dark or light. The result is that you can't do a productive restoration of such a photo because there is nothing blurred in it. (A restoration attempts to "de-blur" a blurred picture.)

What we did do was false color enhance it, and "grey-scale stretch" it on the IPPS viewing system at Kitt Peak. Viewing the photo in this way after densitometerizing it verified our suspicions that there really wasn't extra detail that could be further enhanced out of it. In doing this we found some peculiar vertical stripes in the picture which first we questioned. But then we noticed the original print has a mat surface and this caused the vertical stripes in the picture.

There is one suspicious detail in the picture which merits looking into. When I showed it to a woman who formerly lived at Lake Champlain, she immediately noticed a brownish streak going horizontally from left to right across the picture right up to the object in question. She right out said that it looked to her like a sand bar.

I hadn't noticed it before because there is just a little more brown in that streak than there is in the rest of the picture. But if you rotate the picture clockwise by 90 degrees, then that stripe is vertical and is more apparent to the eye. You see, the eye doesn't discriminate horizontal darknesses on a lake very well because we're so used to seeing horizontal greynesses, so that's why you have to rotate the picture so the vertical position really shows up much better.

I think it's a real detail in the picture because the picture is a very high quality print and it looks like the colors are developed very accurately. I think that the browns that we see there really do belong in the picture. And since they all string together, it certainly looks like a real detail. In other words, it's not an artifact of the development process.

Now if that detail really is there, it has some interesting implications. It might mean there was a sand bar going across. There is another school of thought which says that since it's dark, maybe it means deep water. But I don't think it would be a brownish color if it was deep water—it would be more toward a dark blue. At any rate, if it is a sand bar—and this could be verified by a person who knows lake biology, a limnologist—then there is a distinct possibility that the object was put there by someone, either by the people who took the photo or by the people who were fooling them, because you could simply walk out on such a sand bar and tow the object behind you and hide behind it as you made it rise out of the water and so forth. There'd be a way of hoaxing people, especially if they were frightened out of their wits as these people say they were. Otherwise, the water being as cold as it is, and the object appearing to be so far out as it is — of course that distance has to be verified — it would be very difficult to hoax the object. If it is that far out, it is large; and the water is cold, therefore you'd have to have a wet suit on, real protection from cold water, and it would be a big bother to do such a hoax. But if that is a sand bar then it makes it much easier, the water is shallow and you could pull it out behind you and so forth.

Also, the water would be warm if this is a shallower part, and this is in the daytime. So the sand bar problem really has to be investigated. And you probably don't have to find the actual spot to verify it, you could get an expert on lakes and he could tell from the picture, I believe, if that is a sand bar or not.

Another question posed by this woman who used to live there: She was suspicious that the lake was so narrow at that point because Lake Champlain is colossal in width, and that this would have had to take place at what's called "The Narrows" by the natives who live around there for it to be a true photograph of the area. I say that it's suspicious because if it is an uncharacteristically narrow portion of the lake, perhaps the picture wasn't taken at Lake Champlain but rather at some other body of water.

We have a permanent record of the head, and half of the neck, and just a tiny bit of the back hump. This is recorded on computer punch cards, and I'll be having it in my office for any possible future processing of that data.

To summarize: The picture appears to be a valid print, not a superposition, of a real object somewhere out on a fairly large body of water. There are some interesting things that have to be verified, such as the possibility of the sand bar, and if the sand bar question is resolved and the fact that it's not a sand bar can be really confirmed, then there's much smaller likelihood of this being a hoax.

— *recorded by* J. RICHARD GREENWELL

APPENDIX 3

Cryptozoology, 1, 1982, 54–61

An Estimate of the Dimensions of the Lake Champlain Monster from the Length of Adjacent Wind Waves in the Mansi Photograph

PAUL H. LEBLOND
Department of Oceanography,
The University of British Columbia,
Vancouver, British Columbia V6T 1W5, Canada

ABSTRACT: Empirical results relating the appearance of the sea surface to wind speed and thence to the length of wind waves are used to provide an estimate of the dimensions of "Champ," as seen in the Mansi photograph. Over the possible ranges of wind speed and fetch, lower and upper bounds for the water-line dimension of "Champ" range from 4.8 m to 17.2 m.

Introduction

A PROBLEM which commonly arises in the interpretation of images of unfamiliar objects on water is that of determining their size. In the absence of nearby reference features, the eye cannot estimate absolute dimensions reliably. Too often, even when photographs are available, neither the geometry of the situation nor the optical properties of the camera are known with sufficient accuracy to deduce scales from triangulation. An example in point is the color Instamatic photograph of the Lake Champlain Monster ("Champ") taken by Sandra Mansi in 1977. A sketch based on the photograph appears as Fig. 1. Color reproductions of the original photograph have been published in *Time* (July 13,

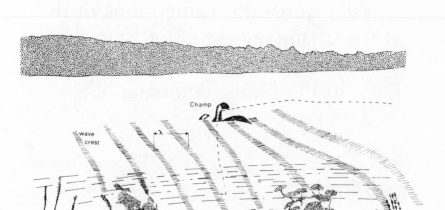

FIG. 1. — A sketch of the Mansi photograph of Champ emphasizing the waves visible at the water surface. See text for explanation of symbols.

1981) and in *Life* (August, 1982); black and white versions have appeared in *The New York Times* (June 30, 1981) and in *The ISC Newsletter* (Vol. 1, No. 2). Neither the features of the far shore, nor the shrubs appearing in the foreground, are suitable as a scale for the object seen in the water.

This paper discusses the use of a different scale, which may sometimes be used in scenes of the water surface. It is shown here how, from the general appearance of the water surface, it may be possible to estimate the length of waves seen thereon, and hence to use the latter as a scale with which to compare objects of uncertain dimensions. The method is applied to the Mansi photograph.

Method

Mariners estimate wind speed from the appearance of the sea surface through the Beaufort scale (Table 1). Each level in that scale is associated with visually distinguishable features of the sea surface. The first step in this method thus consists of deciding on a Beaufort Scale number corresponding to the conditions observed. This step yields a range of possible wind speeds.

The properties of wind waves depend on the speed and duration of the wind, and on the fetch over which it has been blowing. Waves may be fetch-limited or duration-limited, depending on which of these two factors impose a limit on their size. Empirical results relating the significant wave period T_s and wave height H_s to fetch F and wind speed U are given in a number of sources (Wiegel 1964, U.S. Army 1973, Van Dorn 1974). A graphical form of these relations is shown in Fig. 2. Knowing fetch and wind speed, one must first estimate the wind duration t_{min} below which the waves are duration-limited. If the wind has blown for a time $t > t_{min}$, the period T_s and the wave height H_s are read from the appropriate curves as functions of the parameter gF/U^2. Should t be less than t_{min}, however, a shorter fetch F^* is used, related to F through $F^* = Ft/t_{min}$; wave height and period are then calculated from gF^*/U^2.

The wavelength λ depends in general on the water depth D, as well as on wave period T_s. Provided the water is not too shallow, however, i.e., not less than about one third of a wavelength, the depth dependence is unimportant, and one may use the approximate expression (LeBlond and Mysak 1978):

$$\lambda = gT_s^2/2\pi.$$

The final step in the procedure consists of comparing the horizontal extent of the unknown object at the water line with the length of the waves in its immediate vicinity.

Sources of error may appear at many stages of the estimation method, and this must be kept in mind when interpreting the results. First of all, the Beaufort scale determines only a *range* of wind speeds. Secondly, there is some possibility of error in the

TABLE 1. — The Beaufort wind scale and the appearance of the sea at various wind speeds. The scale has been truncated here to the lower wind speeds; continuation to storms and hurricanes may be found in Gross (1977).

Beaufort number	Wind speed (m/sec)	Wind description	Appearance of the water surface
0	0	Calm	Surface like a mirror
1	0.3–1.5	Light air	Ripples with the appearance of scales; no foam crests
2	1.6–3.3	Light breeze	Small wavelets; crests of glassy appearance, no breaking
3	3.4–5.4	Gentle breeze	Large wavelets; crests begin to break; scattered whitecaps
4	5.5–7.9	Moderate breeze	Small waves, becoming longer; numerous whitecaps
5	8.0–10.7	Fresh breeze	Moderate waves, taking longer form; many whitecaps; some spray
6	10.8–13.8	Strong breeze	Large waves begin to form; whitecaps everywhere; more spray
7	13.9–17.1	Near gale	Sea heaps up and white foam from breaking waves begins to be blown in streaks
8	17.2–20.7	Gale	Moderately high waves of greater length; edges of crests begin to break into spindrift; foam is blown in well-marked streaks
9	20.8–24.4	Strong gale	High waves; dense streaks of foam; spray may affect visibility

fetch estimate if the wind direction is not known with certainty, or if the exact position of the observation is not precisely determined. The duration of the wind may not be available, with possible consequences on the effective value of fetch which enters the calculations. Finally, wind waves are quite variable in their length and height, and although the significant wave height and period correspond closely to visually observed wave properties, they are average estimates: individual waves will vary about these averages, and this variability should be taken into account when comparing the dimensions of the object with that of the waves.

Results

THE MAIN features of the Mansi photograph are reproduced in sketch form in Fig. 1. The sketch was drawn from an enlargement of the original print, and emphasizes the principal water waves seen in the field of view. Two main groups of waves are discernible. The dominant waves, in terms of height and length, have crests running nearly perpendicular to shore. The appearance of

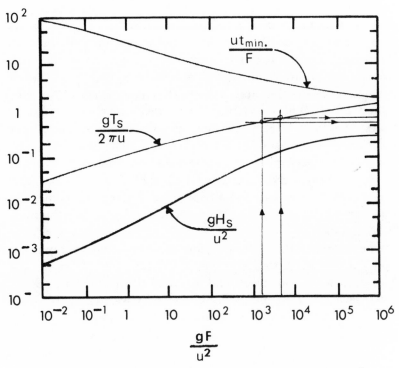

FIG. 2. — Empirical relations between wave properties, wind speed U and fetch F. H_s and T_s are the significant wave height and period respectively; t_{min} is the wind duration below which the waves are duration- rather than fetch-limited. The method of evaluation of T_s from gF/U^2 for the range of F considered in the text and the higher wind speed estimate is sketched in. For greater accuracy, the equation

$$\frac{gT_s}{2\pi U} = 1.2 \tanh[0.077(gF/U^2)^{0.25}]$$

may be used instead of the curve. From Sarpkaya and Isaacson (1981).

147

the wave crests and the position of the few breakers indicate that the waves propagate from left to right. The other group of waves, smaller in height and shorter in length, have crests nearly parallel to shore; they appear to result from the scattering of the wind waves from an irregular shoreline. There is no clear indication of waves produced by Champ itself.

The lower right hand quadrant of the photograph appears lighter than the rest of the lake surface; this area is roughly bounded by the dashed line in Fig. 1. Although it might be argued that this feature reveals the presence of a relatively shallow sandy area in that part of the lake, this hypothesis is inconsistent with the behavior of the waves travelling over that area. In the other parts of the photograph, waves are seen to be breaking at a few isolated spots and the surface shows the characteristics associated with Beaufort Number 3 (Table 1). As waves travel into shallower water, they slow down, steepen, and eventually break. If the paler area corresponded to the presence of a shallow sand bank, one would expect the waves to be modified, and particularly to break more often there than elsewhere. This is not the case, and it seems more reasonable to attribute the different appearance of that part of the lake surface to reflection of light from the overhead clouds.

The exact location from which the Mansi photograph was taken has not been precisely determined. Interviews with Mr. and Mrs. Mansi (R. Greenwell and R. Mackal, priv. comm., Sept., 1982) reveal that the picture looks generally westwards, from the eastern shore of the northeast part of Lake Champlain, north of St. Albans Bay, Vermont, but south of the Canadian border (Fig. 3), and that the Mansis had to walk about 100 meters across a field to gain access to the lake from the road on which they were driving. Roads follow the shoreline on the Vermont side from opposite Butler Is. to Maquam Bay, and along part of the west side of Hog Island. Possible fetches from the southern quadrant thus range from about 5 to 15 km.

Given that possible range of fetches, the parameter gF/U^2 takes values ranging from 4,200 to 21,200 for the lower wind speed estimate (3.4 m/sec), and from 1,700 to 5,000 for the higher wind speed (5.4 m/sec) of Beaufort wind scale 3. From the upper curve of Fig. 2, we find that the range of value of t_{min}, the wind duration below which the waves are duration-limited, is from 1.0 to 3.0 hours for both the lower and the higher wind speed. This duration is short enough that we can assume, in the absence of any other information, that the waves are fetch- and not duration-limited. There is thus no need to correct the fetch, as dis-

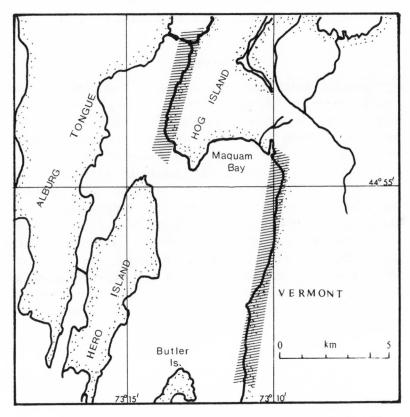

FIG. 3. — The northeast corner of Lake Champlain, from just north of St. Albans Bay, Vermont (below the right hand corner of the map) to the Canadian border, drawn from NOAA map 14781. Stretches of shoreline from which the Mansi photograph may have been taken are shown by a shaded strip.

cussed above, and using the middle curve in Fig. 2, we obtain the periods T_s and (from the equation quoted earlier), the wavelength λ of the fetch-limited waves. For the lower wind speed (U = 3.4 m/sec), λ ranges from 3.2 m to 5.5 m; for the higher wind speed (U = 5.4 m/sec), λ takes values from 5.4 m to 8.6 m, as the fetch increases from 5 to 15 km. Over the whole gamut of expected wind speeds and fetches, the wavelength can range from 3.2 to 8.6 m. From Fig. 1, Champ stretches from 1.5 to 2 wavelengths at the water line: this dimension thus ranges from an extreme lower bound of 4.8 m to an extreme upper bound of 17.2 m.

Discussion

THE RANGE of water line dimensions obtained for Champ is quite broad because the conditions under which the photograph were taken are not known very accurately. If the fetch were known accurately, the ratio of upper to lower bound in wavelength could be reduced by a factor of two. There always remains, however, a range of uncertainty associated with estimating the wind speed through the Beaufort scale, as well as some uncertainty (due to the natural variability of the waves) in determining the scale of the object in term of number of wavelengths.

The inescapable conclusion, nevertheless, is that the object seen in the Mansi photograph is of considerable size. The visual estimate given by Mr. Mansi (15 to 20 feet: 4.6 to 6.1 meters at the waterline) falls within the lower part of the length range estimated here, and provides independent confirmation of this conclusion.

References Cited

Gross, M. G.
  1977 *Oceanography: A View of the Earth* (2nd Ed.). Englewood Cliffs, N.J.: Prentice-Hall.
LeBlond, P. H., and L. A. Mysak
  1978 *Waves in the Ocean*. Amsterdam: Elsevier.

Sarpkaya, T., and M. Isaacson

   1981   *Mechanics of Wave Forces on Offshore Structures.* New York: Van Nostrand Reinhold.

U.S. Army, Corps of Engineers

   1977   *Shore Protection Manual* (3rd Ed.). Coastal Engineering Research Center, Fort Belvoir, Va. Washington, D.C.: U.S. Govt. Printing Office.

Van Dorn, W. G.

   1974   *Oceanography and Seamanship.* New York: Dodd, Mean & Co.

Wiegel, R. L.

   1964   *Oceanographical Engineering.* Englewood Cliffs, N.J.: Prentice-Hall.

Recorded Sightings Of Champ

THIS chart documents and outlines 224 sightings of the Champ phenomenon from 1609–1984. Of these sightings, over 37% represent sightings by eyewitnesses observing Champ's head/neck (this statistic could be higher, but many newspaper recorded sightings only state that the animal was observed, but fail to give details of its morphology). Of those sightings with known dates the breakdown by years is:

1600s–1 1700s–0 1800s–46 1900s–177

Credit goes to hundreds of people for helping to make this chart so complete. Thanks to Connie Pope (formerly a librarian at SUNY/Plattsburgh) for cataloguing and indexing some of the 19th century Champ sightings that were published in local and regional newspapers. And to Dr. Philip Reines for sharing Connie Pope's cataloguing and indexing of these 19th century sightings with me that help to make up part of my chart. These sightings and many other references to Champ are filed for public review at the Special Collections, Feinberg Library, SUNY/Plattsburgh, Plattsburgh, New York. Gary S. Mangiacopra, too, deserves mention for his Champ sighting documentation effort in his two part article: "Lake Champlain: America's Loc Ness"– Spring, 1978 and Summer, 1978 (*Of Sea and Shore*), from which I extracted several Champ sightings of which I was unaware. I would like to acknowledge M.P. Meaney for her indexing assistance and for her aid in proofreading during the compilation of this chart. However, special credit goes to the scores of eyewitnesses I have conversed with via written communications, phone conversations, or face to face interviews. Their observations and sharing of the details of their sightings have significantly added to the Champ data base.

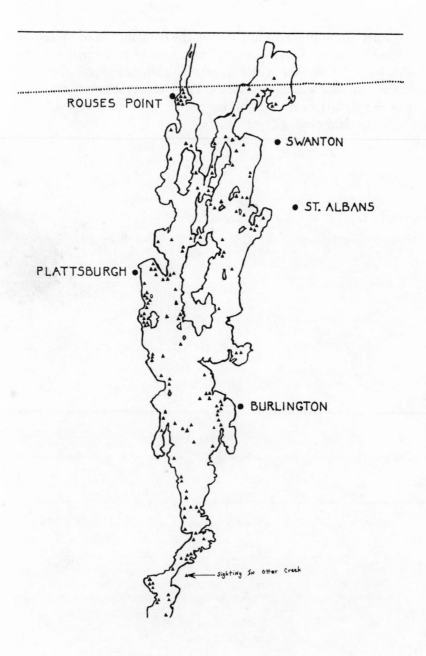

ROUSES POINT

● SWANTON

● ST. ALBANS

PLATTSBURGH ●

● BURLINGTON

← Sighting In Otter Creek

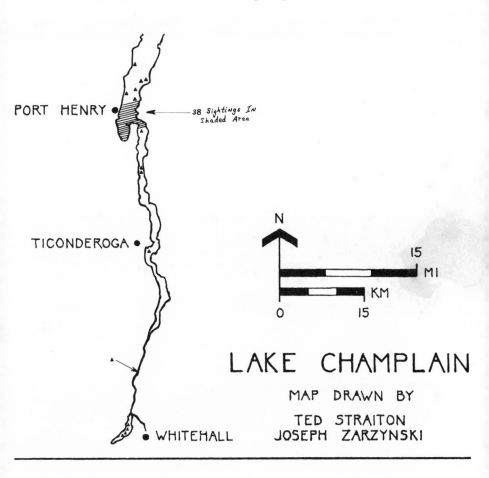

LAKE CHAMPLAIN

MAP DRAWN BY

TED STRAITON
JOSEPH ZARZYNSKI

The sightings plotted on this map represent those recorded up to the May 23, 1984 sighting (sighting #224) when the first edition of this book went to press. Of those 224 catalogued Champ sightings, 198 are plotted on this "Champ Sighting Map." Those not plotted include sightings in which no location was recorded, sightings in which nicknames or archaic names were used to designate a location, and sightings whose location was too generalized by the eyewitness(es) for plotting purposes. For sightings reported from 1984–1987 see Appendix 6. (Map credit: Ted Straiton and Joseph W. Zarzynski)

Sighting	Date	Eyewitness(es)	Location	Time	Weather and Lake Surface Conditions	Range
1	July, 1609	Samuel de Champlain	–	–	–	–
2	July, 1819	Captain Crum	Bulwagga Bay, N.Y.	8 A.M.	–	200 yds
3	Mid 1860s	Mr. Parker	Near White-hall, N.Y.	–	–	–
4	1860s	Mr. Renback Smith, Mr. A.A. Rand	–	–	–	–
5	1860s (?)	Mark Doherty and two other people	South Bay, N.Y.	–	–	50 ft.
6	About 1870	About 50 men working at a quarry	Near Lagoneer Point (?)	–	–	–
7	August, 1871	Passengers of steamer Curlew	Barber Point, N.Y.	–	–	Some distance
8	Summer 1871	–	–	–	–	–
9	July, 1873	Group of people	Dresden, N.Y.	–	–	100 ft.
10	Early 1870s	Mr. John French and family	–	–	Strong South wind	–
11	About 1875	Mr. C.N. Wood, Reverend J.W. Sands	–	–	–	–
12	1877	–	N.Y. side of lake	–	–	–

Eyewitness(es)' Description of Champ	Remarks	Information From:
Some reports state Champlain saw a serpent-like creature 20 ft. long, as thick as a barrel, and a horse shaped head; other reports said he saw a Chaousarou (probably a garfish) some 5 ft. long	This sighting under debate by historians	*Vermont Life* (Summer, 1970) and *The Works* of *Samuel de Champlain* (H.P. Biggar, ed., vol. 2, Toronto, 1925 pgs. 91–92.)
Described as 187 ft. long; head held more than 15 ft. high; head flat with 3 teeth, 2 in center and 1 in upper jaw; head black with white star on forehead; belt of red color around neck; body size of hog's head	Observed from boat (a scow)	*Plattsburgh Republican* (July 24, 1819) – (Possibly July 26, 1819), *Of Sea and Shore* (Spring, 1978), and *Vermont Life* (Summer, 1970)
–	–	*Whitehall Times* (July 30, 1873)
Great size and speed	–	*Plattsburgh Sentinel* (May 6, 1887)
An immense snake, head observed	Observed while fishing from a boat, the sea serpent was trailing a 5 lb. cat-fish the group had hooked	*Whitehall Times* (July 30, 1873)
They thought it was a whale or a big fish	It moved with great speed	*Plattsburgh Sentinel* (May 6, 1887)
Animal going at railroad speed	Observed through a glass	*Vermont Life* (Summer, 1970)
–	Reported by *Vergennes Vermonter*	*Vermont Life* (Summer, 1970)
Travelled at a great speed	Observed by crew and passengers of steamer *W.B. Eddy*	*Whitehall Times* (July 30, 1873)
The monster resembled a large tree with a raised head	It was going with great force and speed into the wind	*Plattsburgh Sentinel* (May 6, 1887)
Log-like, but they believed it to be a living monster	–	*Plattsburgh Sentinel* (May 6, 1887)
–	Supposedly reported in *Essex County Republican* newspaper	*Vermont Life* (Summer, 1970)

Sighting	Date	Eyewitness(es)	Location	Time	Weather and Lake Surface Conditions	Range
13	August 30, 1878	Six people	3/4 mi. west of Button Bay, VT towards Barber Point, N.Y.	–	No ripples on lake surface	1/2 mi.
14	May, 1879	Three St. Albans, VT men (Charles H. Harvey, L.M. Dowing, and W.M. Dowing)	Between Bulter Island and St. Albans, VT shore	After-noon	Dead calm	2 mi.
15	August, 1879	Thomas Johnson	Near west shore of Val-cour Island	–	–	–
16	Septem-ber 15, 1879	Major W.W. Scran-ton and two ladies	Woods Island, VT	–	–	100 ft.
17	Novem-ber, 1879	Three university boys	Burlington Bay, VT. Near Apple-tree Point, VT	–	–	–
18	1870s	Mr. Frederick Fairchild	Near the Boquet River, N.Y.	–	–	–
19	1870s	Group of (New) Yorkers	Horseboat Bay	–	–	–
20	Prob-ably 1870s or 1880s	Mr. and Mrs. John Ferris	Near mouth of Boquet River, N.Y.	–	–	–
21	1800s (pre-1887)	Mr. George French	–	–	–	–
22	July, 1880	Dr. Brigham and another resident of Bedford, Quebec, Canada	Missisquoi Bay, Quebec, Canada	–	–	–

Eyewitness(es)' Description of Champ	Remarks	Information From:
Over 50 ft. long, head visible, several humps visible	Motion of "His Majesty, the Great Snake or Monster of Lake Champlain" was sinuous and undulating	*Plattsburgh Republican* (September 28, 1878) and *Mysterious America* by Loren Coleman
10–12 ft. long, 1–2 ft. in diameter, dark in color	Observed while fishing, the water near the Champlain Sea Serpent lashed into foam and was thrown 30 or 40 ft. high	*Plattsburgh Republican* (May 17, 1879) and *Plattsburgh Sentinel* (May 16, 1879)
About 10 ft. of huge serpent showing, head six in. in diameter, body as thick as a man's	Observed from a boat	*Plattsburgh Republican* (August 16, 1879)
3 or 4 ft. of body length visible, head about the thickness of a man's, dark in color	Observed while boating	*Of Sea and Shore* (Spring, 1978)
15 ft. of length showing	Observed while boating	*Burlington Free Press* (November 7, 1879) and *New York Times* (November 10, 1879)
Looked like a large Newfoundland dog	–	*Plattsburgh Sentinel* (May 6, 1887)
–	Observed during a steamboat excursion from Essex, N.Y.	*Vermont Life* (Summer, 1970)
Monstrous	–	*Plattsburgh Sentinel* (May 6, 1887)
Monstrous	Observed while fishing, described as frightful, but not dangerous	*Plattsburgh Sentinel* (May 6, 1887)
Portions of strange monster's body fully 20 ft. long, head as large as a flour barrel, eyes with greenish tinge	The strange creature made sound in moving that sounded like a steam yacht's paddle wheel	*Swanton Courier* (July 31, 1880)

Sighting	Date	Eyewitness(es)	Location	Time	Weather and Lake Surface Conditions	Range
23	About 1881	Daughter of local minister and Mr. Warren Rockwell	Swanton, VT	–	–	–
24	Autumn 1882	Mr. and Mrs. George Wilkins	Near Willsboro Bay, N.Y.	–	–	–
25	August, 1883	–	Near St. Albans Bay, VT	–	–	–
26	August, 1883	–	Charlotte, VT	–	–	–
27	Summer 1883	Captain Nathan H. Mooney	Cumberland Bay, N.Y. (just past the Head)	4:30 P.M.	Clouds and sun, rough "seas"	50 yds.
28	About 1883	Dr. P.A. Wheeler	Off west shore of North Hero, VT–just south of bridge	–	–	5 rods
29	January, 1886 (?)	E. Brown and several others	Appletree Point, VT	–	–	–
30	July, 1886	George Atwood and friend	Near mouth of Dead Creek, VT	Morn-ing	Sunny	–
31	August, 1886	Three men	Cumberland Bay, N.Y.	7 A.M.	Very calm, sunny	20 rods
32	August, 1886	An Essex, N.Y. man (name unknown)	–	–	–	–

Eyewitness(es)' Description of Champ	Remarks	Information From:
Animal	Viewed from the rear deck of a steamboat; the steamboat pilot, Mr. Warren Rockwell, shot at it when it finally disappeared	*Plattsburgh Republican* (May 21, 1887)
–	–	*Plattsburgh Sentinel* (May 6, 1887)
–	–	*Vermont Life* (Summer, 1970)
Animal	–	*Vermont Life* (Summer, 1970)
25 ft. long, 7 in. in diameter, head at least 4 or 5 ft. above water, neck muscles contracted and neck curved, head flattened and triangular, nose forming sharp v-shaped angle	Captain Mooney was Sheriff of Clinton County, N.Y. Sighting took place while onboard the boat, *Nellie*	*Plattsburgh Republican* (August 4, 1883) and *Vermont Life* (Summer, 1970)
Head was 3-4 ft. out of water, head was 8-10 in. in diameter, eyes visible, dark in color	Animal lashing in shallow water near shore until it swam off	*Plattsburgh Republican* (May 21, 1887)
Looked like a steam yacht at a great distance, however it moved at a pace 4 times the speed of any yacht, white in color	Observed from shore	*Of Sea and Shore* (Spring, 1978)
14 ft. out of water, head visible, red tongue, eyes glowed wildly, teeth visible, horns, whalebone mane, scales, color – handsome drab with white points and a gold belly	Observed from boat *Hattie Bell* just before fishing	*Plattsburgh Morning Telegram* (July 13, 1886) and *Burlington Free Press* (July 16, 1886)
15 ft. long, head about 15-18 in. in length, head raised 2 ft. above water	–	*Plattsburgh Morning Telegram* (August 14, 1886)
20 ft. long, huge snake, eel type head, body as large as a man's and snake-like, tail shaped like an eel's	Observed from railway tracks above lake	*Plattsburgh Morning Telegram* (January 26, 1887)

Sighting	Date	Eyewitness(es)	Location	Time	Weather and Lake Surface Conditions	Range
33	Summer 1886	–	Keeseville, N.Y.	–	–	–
34	November, 1886	E. Brown	Near Four Brothers (north of these islands)	Afternoon	Pleasant and still, but light breeze and very small ripples on lake	–
35	December 1, 1886	Mr. S.W. Clark and others	1 mile east of Willsboro Point, N.Y.	Noon	Windy and "light seas"	1 mi.
36	1886 (?)	D. Brown	West side of Willsboro Point, N.Y.	Just before dark	–	10–15 rods
37	May 3, 1887 (?)	Workers from Port Henry Ore & Iron Company and the Lake Champlain & Moriah Railroad Company	Going into Bullwagga (Bulwagga) Bay, N.Y.	–	–	–
38	July, 1887	A group of picnic people from Charlotte, VT	–	Afternoon	–	–
39	August 20, 1887	Party of five from Charlotte, VT	Opposite Deer Point	–	No wind, lake surface perfectly motionless	60 rods
40	Summer 1887	Mr. Lewis Smith	–	2 P.M.	–	1 mi.
41	Summer 1887	A fishing party	North of Split Rock ore bed, N.Y.	–	–	–
42	May 18, 1887 (?)	Mr. Winford Morhous, Mr. and Mrs. Hiram Morhous, and their hired girl	East of Willsboro Point, N.Y. (just north of Four Brothers)	6:30 P.M.	–	–

Eyewitness(es)' Description of Champ	Remarks	Information From:
—	—	*Essex County Republican* (September 2, 1886)
Sudden commotion on flat water, it would roll then disappear	—	*Of Sea and Shore* (Spring, 1978)
Dark body	They used small spyglass to view animal	*Plattsburgh Sentinel* (December 10, 1886), *Plattsburgh Republican* (December 11, 1886) and *Vermont Life* (Summer, 1970)
Like a long log or pole	Observed while out in a boat	*Of Sea and Shore* (Spring, 1978)
Claimed they saw the Champlain Sea Serpent	—	Notes from Connie Pope (Newspaper source – ?, May 14, 1887)
50–75 ft. long, body as large as a barrel, a flat serpent-like head, motions in the lake's water like the undulations of a snake's body	A minister present at the sighting stated the picnickers had no beverages stronger than milk and lemonade	*Plattsburgh Republican* (July 16, 1887)
15–20 ft. long, head and tail visible, snake-like form	Observed from rowboat	*Plattsburgh Morning Telegram* (August 29, 1887)
Size of a barrel, the height of a man, a dark head, colored white below the water	The animal made a noise like a steamboat	*Plattsburgh Sentinel* (May 6, 1887)
Observed sea serpent	Observed while fishing	*Plattsburgh Sentinel* (August 5, 1887)
Head of animal observed	Its speed was much faster than the fastest steamboats	*Plattsburgh Sentinel* (May 27, 1887)

Sighting	Date	Eyewitness(es)	Location	Time	Weather and Lake Surface Conditions	Range
43	September, 1889	Party from Shelburn(e), VT	Near Juniper Island, VT	–	–	A few rods distant
44	August 4, 1892	Some members of the American Canoe Association	–	–	–	–
45	1892	Captain Moses Blow	2½ mi. north of Basin Harbor, VT	2 P.M.	Serene day	–
46	September, 1894	Luther Hager, Tim Miller, Frank Dominy, Ephraim Allen	Southern tip of Cumberland Head, N.Y. (opposite reef)	Afternoon	–	20 rods
47	Summer 1899	"A wealthy New Yorker"	Between Split Rock, N.Y. and VT	–	–	–
48	About 1900	Henry Washburn and son, Carl	Malletts Bay, VT	–	–	–
49	April 14, 1915	Several local inhabitants	Entrance of Bulwagga Bay, N.Y.	–	–	–
50	1918	Frank Burrough	South Bay, N.Y.	–	Calm bay	–
51	July, 1937	Gene McGabe, Coots Gordon, Pat Harvey	Whitehall, N.Y.	–	–	–
52	July 15, 1936 or 1937	Captain Johnny Blair and a deckhand	Chimney Point, VT	–	–	–

Eyewitness(es)' Description of Champ	Remarks	Information From:
15 ft. of creature visible, head well out of water, many large fins	Observed while fishing, the party gave chase until the sea serpent disappeared	*Essex County Republican* (September 26, 1889) and *Plattsburgh Sentinel* (September 27, 1889)
—	While at their annual outing, some members of the American Canoe Association saw the animal rise up in the middle of their flotilla of canoes. . . scattering the group of canoes	*Monsters Among Us: Journey to the Unexplained* by John Lee and Barbara Moore, *Ithaca Journal* (February 15, 1971), *Vermont Life* (Summer, 1970), and *Mysterious America* by Loren Coleman
Body appeared long, but stayed below the water, long neck and a serpent's head, gray in color	Observed from stern of boat, the *A. Williams*	From a letter to *Burlington Free Press* (December 11, 1975)
Dark on top and lighter in appearance close to water	The animal was reported to have gone 6 ft. or more out of water and onto land	*Essex County Republican* (September 27, 1894) and *Vermont Life* (Summer, 1970)
35 ft. long, head like an inverted platter, back arched, broad flat tail raised several feet out of water	Animal swimming slowly	*Plattsburgh Republican* (August 5, 1899)
—	Observed while fishing in a rowboat	*Vermont Life* (Summer, 1970)
40 ft. long	Observed with field glasses	*New York Times* (April 19, 1915) and *The North Countryman* (December 12, 1968)
Ridge of fins 15 ft. long on back, round head with jaws like an alligator, skin smooth	—	Letter from Mrs. Doris Morton (Town Historian—Whitehall, N.Y.)
About 50 ft. long, flowing red mane, dinner-plate eyes, moose-like antlers, elephant ears	Observed while fishing from a lake pier	From a Syracuse, N.Y. based newspaper (July 22, 1937)
60 ft. long, 8 ft. high, sharp scales along its back, broad large flappers, hard skin	Observed from an "oil tanker," the creature blew like a whale	From a Syracuse, N.Y. based newspaper (July 22, 1937)

Sighting	Date	Eyewitness(es)	Location	Time	Weather and Lake Surface Conditions	Range
53	August, 1939	Couple (two people)	Rouses Point, N.Y.	–	–	–
54	(1920s or 1930s)	Elsie Porter and her brother	Near Port Kent, N.Y.	–	–	–
55	July, 1940	Robert Hughes	Plattsburgh, N.Y. military barracks	Between midnight and 2 A.M.	Breezy with some ripples on lake surface	120 ft.
56	1943	Charles Weston	Rouses Point, N.Y.	–	–	–
57	1945	Mr. and Mrs. Charles Langlois	Near Rouses Point, N.Y.	–	–	See Remarks
58	1945	–	–	–		–
59	1945	Passengers aboard the S.S. Ticonderoga	–	–	–	–
60	June 25, 1946	Mrs. Henry G. Augins, H.G. Augins, Mr. and Mrs. Martin Davis, Mr. and Mrs. Fred Chevalier	Near Rouses Point, N.Y. (?)	Evening	–	–
61	Mid 1940s	Miss Minerva Sloughton and others	Cumberland Head, N.Y. (looking toward Grand Isle, VT)	–	Fine weather	–

Eyewitness(es)' Description of Champ	Remarks	Information From:
—	The animal surfaced and then began looping its way toward the boat	*Vermont Life* (Summer, 1970)
As big as a rhinoceros' back when it came up, 3 humps, humps like a camel only more pointed, head like an anaconda or boa constrictor, black or brown in color. . .dark. . .it could have been dark green	Observed many times, info from a tape played by Dr. Reines at the "Does Champ Exist?" Seminar	"Does Champ Exist?" Seminar Proceedings (August 29, 1981)
Head/neck and hump visible	Observed while on military guard duty	Letter from Robert Hughes (May 20, 1980) and completed sighting sheet from Robert Hughes (May 23, 1980)
Animal or huge reptile	Observed with binoculars, the animal churned up water	*Mysterious America* by Loren Coleman and *Vermont Life* (Summer, 1970)
15–20 ft. long and thick as a keg	The Langlois couple said they came close enough to it in their rowboat to "whack it with an oar"	*Monsters Among Us: Journey To The Unexplained* by John Lee and Barbara Moore, *Ithaca Journal* (February 15, 1971) and *Vermont Life* (Summer, 1970)
—	"Baby Sea Serpent Taken In Vermont Waters—May be Offspring of Lake Monster"	*Vermont Life* (Summer, 1970)
Head visible	Observed when vessel was in center of lake while passengers observed a bridge-opening ceremony	*Monsters Among Us: Journey to the Unexplained* by John Lee and Barbara Moore and *Ithaca Journal* (February 15, 1971)
18–20 ft. in length	Mrs. Henry G. Augins saw the head of animal (she was the only one in the party to do so)	*The Essex County Republican* (July 5, 1946)
Dark colored	—	*Vermont Life* (Summer, 1970)

Sighting	Date	Eyewitness(es)	Location	Time	Weather and Lake Surface Conditions	Range
62	September 10, 1947	L.R. Jones and two companions	Off northern tip of North Hero Island, VT	6 P.M.	Calm and clear	300 yds.
63	June 12, 1949	Mr. and Mrs. Harold Taylor, Mrs. Paul Narreau	Alburg Bay, VT	–	–	100 ft., then saw it as it was under-water but close up
64	July, 1950	–	Dead Creek/ Missisquoi Bay, VT	–	–	80 ft.
65, 66, 67	1951	Mrs. Theresa Megargee (her husband had a sighting the second time she saw it)	Opposite Valcour Island, N.Y.	–	–	–
68	July, 1952	Joseph Hubbard and family	Near mouth of the Winooski River, VT	–	–	–
69	1952	Two ladies	Malletts Bay, VT	–	–	–

Eyewitness(es)' Description of Champ	Remarks	Information From:
Overall length about 25 ft., 3 segments (dark) separated one from each other by 5 ft. of water	Observed while the 3 people were fishing, the animal moved about 15 m.p.h. and disappeared in about 2 minutes	*Burlington Free Press* (September 20, 1947) and *Vermont Life* (Summer, 1970)
6 ft. in length and as big around as a man, 300–400 lbs. in weight	Described as possibly being a large sturgeon about 6 ft. long	*The North Countryman* (June 16, 1949)
18–20 ft. long, dark gray in color	Sighting by a friend of Daniel McNally, the friend is now deceased	Letter from Daniel McNally (January 10, 1982)
"I would say length to be more 30 ft. rather than 20 ft."–Mrs. Theresa Megargee	Mrs. Theresa Megargee claimed three sightings in one year; she believes it may be an ocean sturgeon (Atlantic sturgeon), the third time Mrs. Megargee "shot at it with an old, octagon-barreled .30–40 Winchester rifle." She wrote, "At the time, I thought my beautiful baby might one day be a tempting 'hors d'oeuvre', and I was a protective young mother."	Letters from Mrs. Theresa Megargee (September 22, 1980 and November 25, 1980) and *Adirondack Life* (May/June 1982, p. 56)
6–7 ft. long and perhaps 2 ft. wide, tan or gray fringe or mane from its head along top and bottom, black and gray in color, no tail	Observed while casting from a boat, Joseph Hubbard thought it was chasing a Northern Pike in shallow water	*Burlington Free Press* (July 10, 1952) and *Vermont Life* (Summer, 1970)
—	Observed while fishing	*Vermont Life* (Summer, 1970)

Sighting	Date	Eyewitness(es)	Location	Time	Weather and Lake Surface Conditions	Range
70	1954	A high school principal and three other men	Between Swanton, VT and Alburg, VT	–	–	–
71	Summer 1955	Mrs. Mary C. Krom, husband, daughter, and a friend	Off Grand Isle, VT	Twi-light, after dinner	Very hot and dry weather	25 ft.
72	Approx-imately 1950 (Other accounts indicate mid 1960s)	Dr. Donald B. Mears	West side of South Hero Island, VT	4 P.M.	–	300 ft.
73	May 20, 1960	Mr. and Mrs. Harold Patch	Dillenback Bay, Alburg, VT	12 Noon	Lake like a mirror	300 yds.
74	Labor Day, 1960 or 1962	Mr. and Mrs. Walter Hard	Appletree Point, Burlington, VT	After-noon	After a thunderstorm, choppy water	100 yds. offshore
75	Spring 1961	Thomas E. Morse	North West Bay, N.Y.	After-noon	Slightly overcast	–
76	Octo-ber, 1961	Mr. and Mrs. Walter Foley	Between Hogback and Providence Islands, VT	6:45 P.M.	–	Less than ¼ mi.

Eyewitness(es)' Description of Champ	Remarks	Information From:
20 ft. long, like a telephone pole in appearance	Observed while fishing from a boat	*Vermont Life* (Summer, 1970)
The part observed was 6 ft. long with a wide back, shiny surface, black in color	Observed while out in a rowboat	Letter from Mrs. Mary C. Krom (September 21, 1979)
Considerable size, head visible (looked like a big snake), black in color	Observed while cruising on the lake	*Strange Secrets Of The Loch Ness Monster* by Warren Smith and *National Enquirer* (May 2, 1971)
20 ft., head raised 2-3 ft. above water, body rose vertically in several loops, darkish gray in color	They used a 7 × 35 pair of binoculars to observe the animal for approximately ½ hour	Interview with Harold Patch (June 13, 1976)
20-25 ft. in length, 2-3 humps, globular, dirty white head looked like an old bathing cap, body appeared reddish brown in color	Observed with field glasses, "We saw something out there that was definitely larger than any fish. It didn't fit the description of anything I'd seen or heard before. As far as I'm concerned there is some kind of marine monster in Lake Champlain." —Walter Hard	*Vermont Life* (Summer, 1970) and *Albany Times-Union* (November 23, 1975)
30-50 ft. long, eel-like, 18 in. wide, gray in color	Observed from car while student-driving, the animal crawled out of water onto shore	Letter from Thomas E. Morse (September 20, 1980) and completed sighting sheet from Thomas E. Morse (October 8, 1980)
2 sections of creature visible moving up and down	Observed while fishing, "To us it looked like a huge snake."—Mrs. Foley	*Burlington Free Press* (October 11, 1961)

Sighting	Date	Eyewitness(es)	Location	Time	Weather and Lake Surface Conditions	Range
77	1961	Ray C. Pecor and family, Sally Clerkin	Shelburne, VT	6 P.M.	–	–
78	Around Summer 1962	–	Westport, N.Y.	–	–	–
79	July, 1964	Joan Weissbecker, Mrs. Jud Ellenwood, and others	Barber's Bay, Westport, N.Y.	After-noon	Calm, mild, sunshine	–
80	July, 1966	(Eyewitness requested his name remain anonymous)	Campbell's Bay near Missisquoi Bay, VT (1 mile from Canada)	–	Calm, glass-like water	200 ft.
81	July, 1965 or July, 1966	Anne P. Marsh	Whallon Bay, N.Y., near Split Rock	Late after-noon	–	–
82	Mid 1960s	Martha B. Kneeshaw and daughter	Panton, VT	Hour before sun-down	–	¼ mi.
83	Mid 1960s	Avril Trudeau and friend	Swanton, VT (off Maquam shore and towards Butler Island, VT)	Early morn-ing	Hot, muggy, very calm lake surface	50 ft. and more
84	Early Spring 1967	Gordon F. Baker	Bulwagga Bay, N.Y.	7 A.M.	Sunshine, lake like glass	50 ft.
85	1967	J. Tremblay and brother-in-law	West side of Missisquoi Bay on Canadian – USA border	–	Balmy, lake sur-face like glass	50 ft.

172

Eyewitness(es)' Description of Champ	Remarks	Information From:
12 ft. long, grayish in color	It reminded Mr. Pecor of whales he had seen in the Pacific Ocean	*Burlington Free Press* (August 28, 1961)
—	Sightings reported by Alex Boisseau	*Vermont Life* (Summer, 1970)
Several humps, scaly, body diameter about 8 in., head size of grapefruit	—	Letter from Frank Weissbecker (September 14, 1978), letter from Mrs. Jud Ellenwood (November 10, 1978), and *Vermont Life* (Summer, 1970)
20–25 ft. long, a large snake, 3 humps, no head or tail seen, dark in color	Observed while fishing	Interview with eyewitness (April 6, 1978)
15–18 ft. long, coils, snake-like head, black in color	Animal swimming slowly	Letter from Anne P. Marsh (July 15, 1978)
10–12 ft. long	—	Letter from Martha B. Kneeshaw (June 1, 1978) and interview (July 1, 1978)
An ostrich or duck-like face, head held 3–4 ft. out of water, neck 1½ ft. thick, whiskers, fuzzy head, gray brown in color	Observed from a motorboat, several sightings over a 2 hour period	Letter from Avril Trudeau (July 3, 1981)
Over 20 ft. long, greenish gray in color	Observed while fishing from boat	Completed sighting sheet from Gordon F. Baker (October 7, 1980)
25 ft. long, 3 humps, smooth skin, grayish in color	Observed from a 16 ft. long boat while trolling	From cassette tape by J. Tremblay

173

Sighting	Date	Eyewitness(es)	Location	Time	Weather and Lake Surface Conditions	Range
86	July, 1968	Elizabeth M. Lamica and husband	Off Crown Point bridge	–	Clear and sunny	–
87	Autumn 1960s or 1970s	N.Y.S. trooper, Tony Lemza	Bulwagga Bay, N.Y.	9:30 A.M.	–	1/3 way across Bulwagga Bay
88	June, early 1970s	Ralph Doucet, Burnham G. Gage	West side of Long Point, VT	2 or 3 P.M.	Sunshine, calm lake surface	350 yds. or more
89	Early 1970s	Rosalee McManus and several others	Burlington, VT	Around 4–5 P.M.	Water was still	Close
90	May 17, 1970	Mrs. Grace Lee and several others	Off Isle La Motte bridge, VT	–	–	–
91	July, 1970	Darrell R. Tucker and sister	Addison, VT	6 P.M.	Rain had just stopped, very humid and somewhat foggy	200 yds.
92	Late July, 1970	Anne P. Marsh and several others	Between Essex, N.Y. and Charlotte, VT	–	–	–
93	August, 1970	William Bianchi, Edward F. Taylor	West off Cumberland Head, N.Y.	Around 11 P.M.–midnight	Warm, clear, stars out, some moonlight	60–80 yds.
94	Summer 1970	Edward A. Manship, Jr. and 2–3 others	1.5 mi. off Burlington, VT. breakwater towards Appletree Point, VT	Mid day	Partly cloudy, calm water	300 ft.

Eyewitness(es)' Description of Champ	Remarks	Information From:
35–40 ft. long, 6 ft. wide, head and neck 8 or 10 ft. out of water, body was reddish bronze in color, eyes black with green around them	Observed while crossing Crown Point bridge in vehicle	Letter from Elizabeth M. Lamica (January 28, 1980) and completed sighting sheet (February 8, 1980)
25–30 ft. long, dark in color	Observed from house overlooking Bulwagga Bay	Interview with Tony Lemza (July 7, 1976)
15–20 ft. long, black–dark in color	Reportedly it swam like a snake	Letter and completed sighting sheet from Burnham G. Gage (December 2, 1981)
Over 20 ft. long, huge rounded back, dark brown or black in color	Observed while fishing from shore	Letter from Rosalee McManus (July 21, 1978) and phone interview (June 28, 1978)
3 humps visible with a head shaped like an eel or snake, dark-greenish black	Observed while fishing from a boat	*Burlington Free Press* (May 6, 1971)
10–12 ft. long, 2–3 ft. height out of water, black in color	Observed from D.A.R. State Park	Letter from Darrell R. Tucker (July 24, 1980) and completed sighting sheet from Darrell R. Tucker (August 1, 1980)
15–18 ft. long, coils, snake-like head, black in color	Animal observed from deck of ferry going between Essex, N.Y. and Charlotte, VT; animal swimming slowly; observed with binoculars	Letter from Anne P. Marsh (July 15, 1978)
2 portions sighted 10–15 ft. long, 12–18 in. in diameter, shiny black in color	1, possibly 2 creatures observed according to William Bianchi	Completed sighting sheet from William Bianchi (January 15, 1983) and completed sighting sheet from Edward Taylor (April 23, 1983)
40–60 ft. long, 2–3 ft. wide, up to 1 ft. out of water, smooth skin, dark green or black in color	Observed from ferry crossing lake, observed by naked eye and binoculars	Completed sighting sheet from Edward A. Manship, Jr. (August 3, 1980)

Sighting	Date	Eyewitness(es)	Location	Time	Weather and Lake Surface Conditions	Range
95	September, 1970	Eight people from Isle La Motte, VT	Off east shore of Isle La Motte, VT	Approximately 7– 7:30 P.M.	–	About ½ mi.
96	February 27, 1971	Some townspeople of Port Henry, N.Y.	Port Henry, N.Y.	–	Cold	–
97	August 13, 1971	Berenice Keefe, Jack Grace	Jackson Point, west shore of Grand Isle, VT	10:30 A.M.	Beautiful calm day	No more than 10 ft. from cliffs in front of their camp
98	September 12, 1971	Captain Henry F. Wiseman and wife	Potash Bay, VT	About 3:30 P.M.	Clear, sunshine, calm	250 ft.
99	Autumn 1971	Vincent and Dawn Iamunno	Valcour Island, N.Y.	Late morning	Cloudy, calm lake surface	250– 300 yds.
100	1971 or 1972	Dick Sherman, John Genier	Bulwagga Bay, N.Y.	8 A.M.	–	300–400 yds.
101	Autumn 1971 (or October, 1975)	Richard E. Gilbo, Walter F. Wojewodzic	Bulwagga Bay, N.Y.	10 A.M.	Lake surface calm as glass	300 yds.
102	September, 1971 (?)	Mrs. Robert A. Green and two others	–	Afternoon	Calm	–
103	May, 1972	Fred Shanafelt, Morris Lucia	Maquam Bay and St. Albans Bay, VT vicinity	After breakfast	–	–

Eyewitness(es)' Description of Champ	Remarks	Information From:
20–50 ft. long	Reported to have travelled in mid channel faster than a speedboat	*Burlington Free Press* (September 24, 1970)
–	Reportedly the creature broke through the ice near Velez Marina and then returned under the ice	*Glens Falls Post Star and Times* (March 8, 1971)
25 or 30 ft. long, black in color, round head and arched neck	"This creature was traveling at a great speed."– Berenice Keefe	Letter from Berenice Keefe (January 10, 1977) and completed sighting sheet from Berenice Keefe (January 25, 1977)
9–10 ft. long, back 2–2½ ft. in width, just breaking water, greenish brown in color	Observed twice with 45 minute duration between, animal swimming at 5 knots	Completed sighting sheet from Wisemans (February 9, 1980)
50–75 ft. long, 15 ft. in width, 6–10 ft. in height, smooth surface, grayish in color	Observed while driving in car on Rt. 9	Completed sighting sheet from Iamunnos (January 16, 1981)
Several humps	Observed while working on a restaurant overlooking Bulwagga Bay	Interview with Dick Sherman (July 7, 1976) and interview with John Genier (July 7, 1976)
3 humps, 40 ft. long or more, about 3 ft. high, gray in color	Observed while putting up duck blind	Completed sighting sheet from Richard E. Gilbo and Walter F. Wojewodzic (September 30, 1980)
Super long thing with three humps	–	*Baltimore Sun* (December 9, 1971)
40–50 ft. long, head looked like a horse and was mushroom gray, neck about 8 ft. above water, neck was dark brown or black	Observed from boat after scuba diving	*Strange Secrets Of The Loch Ness Monster* by Warren Smith

Sighting	Date	Eyewitness(es)	Location	Time	Weather and Lake Surface Conditions	Range
104	June, 1972	Barry James Jarrett	Rock Point, VT	Afternoon	Sun shining, smooth lake surface	40 yds.
105	June, 1972 (day after Jarrett's first sighting)	Barry James Jarrett	Rock Point, VT	Approximately 7:45 A.M.	–	–
106	August or September, 1972 or 1973	Elizabeth M. Lamica, Mrs. Eugene Bennett, and Elizabeth Ann Bennett	Off Crown Point bridge	–	Clear and warm sunny day	–
107	1972 or 1973	John F. Durant and his father	North of Essex, N.Y.	–	–	–
108	July, 1973	Gretna Longware and about 15–18 other people	North West Bay, N.Y.	Morning	–	200 yds.
109	August, 1973	Joan, Barbara, and Ray Williams	The Gut, VT	–	Calm lake surface, clear and sunshine	¼ mi.
110	Summer 1973	Louis Velez, Mike Atner, and others	Port Henry, N.Y.	7 P.M.	–	–
111	Summer 1973	Christina and Philip Putnam	Trembleau Point between Keeseville, N.Y. and Port Kent, N.Y.	Late afternoon	Very calm surface	35 ft.
112	Summer 1973	Edward A. Manship, Jr.	3 mi. north from Essex, N.Y.	–	Fairly sunny, calm day	500 yds.

Eyewitness(es)' Description of Champ	Remarks	Information From:
Over 60 ft. in length, 5 coils above surface, horse-like head, head held 7 ft. above surface, eyes deep reddish brown	Observed while in rubber raft, Mr. Jarrett believed he saw a reptile-like creature	Letter from Barry James Jarrett (Spring, 1981)
Same as previous day's sighting	Observed while fishing from shore	Letter from Barry James Jarrett (Spring, 1981)
35-40 ft. long, width was approximately 4 ft., head and neck viewed	Observed while crossing Crown Point bridge in vehicle	Letter from Elizabeth M. Lamica (January 28, 1980) and completed sighting sheet (February 8, 1980)
3 humps, gray	Seen at first by naked eye then through binoculars, observed while boating	Interview with John F. Durant (July 7, 1976)
Described Champ sighting as with a gray dorsal fin	Sighting off marina in Westport, N.Y. on a Sunday morning	*Albany Times-Union* (November 23, 1975)
20 ft. long, snake-like head, 3-4 ft. high, black or dark green in color	Observed from boat by naked eye and with binoculars	Completed sighting sheet from Joan Williams (January 30, 1980)
At least 18-20 ft. long, observed a hump or wake that left a 2 ft. wake, dark or black in color	Louis Velez and others boarded a 14 ft. long boat with a 10 h.p. outboard motor and chased the animal until it dove off Crab Harbor	*Albany Times-Union* (November 23, 1975)
16-18 ft. long, head raised like a periscope, black in color	Observed from canoe	Letter from Putnams (October 18, 1978)
40-60 ft. long, 2-3 ft. wide, up to 1 ft. out of water, smooth skin	Observed from ferry crossing lake	Completed sighting sheet from Edward A. Manship, Jr. (August 3, 1980)

Sighting	Date	Eyewitness(es)	Location	Time	Weather and Lake Surface Conditions	Range
113	October, 1973	Christine Breyette	–	Around 4–5 P.M.	Fairly nice weather	–
114	Autumn 1973	Bill MacBrien	–	–	–	5 yds.
115	July, 1974	Raymond A. Jewett and two friends	Midlake, Willsboro, N.Y.– Shelburne, VT	1 hour before sunset	Clear and relatively calm lake surface	100–200 yds.
116	November, 1974	Lynn Webster, Ted Wild	Cumberland Bay, N.Y.	Late afternoon	–	100 yds.
117	June, 1975	Mr. and Mrs. Lenus Drinkwine	1½ mi. north of Port Henry, N.Y.	–	Sunshine, calm lake surface	½ mi.
118	August, 1975	Thomas and Louis Trepasso	Near Button Bay, VT	Morning	foggy	150 ft.
119	August, 1975	C.W. Putnam	Port Henry, N.Y.	Afternoon	Warm weather and water surface was calm	About 4 ft.
120	Summer 1975	Robert Blye and others	Bulwagga Bay, N.Y.	–	Calm	½ to ⅓ mi.
121	September, 1975	Mrs. John Grigas and three others	Seen from rear deck of ferry from Plattsburgh, N.Y. to VT	11 A.M.	–	200–300 ft.

Eyewitness(es)' Description of Champ	Remarks	Information From:
Appeared to be longer, wider, and a darker color gray than a porpoise	Observed while flying in a small airplane going from South to North over the lake	Letters from Christine Breyette (July 13, 1978 and July 22, 1978)
Looked like a submarine periscope, no eyes but a hole in middle of head, 12–18 in. high, leathery or scaly surface, olive-brown in color	Observed from a ferry crossing Lake Champlain	*Fate* (September, 1983)
10–15 ft. long	Observed from a boat	Letter from Raymond A. Jewett (February 6, 1980) and completed sighting sheet from Raymond A. Jewett (February 19, 1980)
Head visible—something that resembled a stove pipe, no dorsal fin	–	Letter from Lynn Webster (December 8, 1977) and letter from Ted Wild (January 3, 1978)
30 ft. long, 3 ft. in height out of water, very dark in color	Observed while driving car north along lake	Completed sighting sheet from the Drinkwines (January 27, 1981)
Two dark objects about 3 ft. high and 4 ft. apart	Observed from boat	Interview with Thomas Trepasso (July 7, 1976)
Sighting compared to a Fla. manatee in appearance, about 4 in. of animal above water, scaleless skin, gray in color	Observed from hovercraft	Letter from C.W. Putnam (July 22, 1978)
20 or 30 ft. long, 2 humps with head not visible, dark in color	Observed from Robert Blye's Restaurant overlooking Bulwagga Bay	Interview with Robert Blye (July 12, 1976) and *Albany Times-Union* (November 23, 1975)
Dog's head and two humps	"We all said, 'What is that thing—It's not a fish—Looks like a dog's head from the distance—Couldn't be a sea otter—too big—Couldn't figure out what it was until we read in the paper some months later about the "sea monster." Had never heard of it before.'"	Letter from Mrs. John Grigas (July 24, 1976)

Sighting	Date	Eyewitness(es)	Location	Time	Weather and Lake Surface Conditions	Range
122	October 23, 1975	Janet Tyler	North West Bay, N.Y.	–	Lake surface calm as glass	–
123	1975	J. Tremblay with his father and mother	Near Rock River, VT	–	Balmy, lake surface smooth as could be	20 ft.
124	October, 1976	Nancy Warren and family	Between Corlear Bay and Willsboro, N.Y.	5:30 P.M.	Bright, clear, sunshine, very calm lake surface	5/8 mi.
125	1976	Orville Wells	Treadwell Bay, N.Y.	Between 1–3 P.M.	Lake surface-ripples	300 yds.
126, 127, 128	Twice in June, 1977 and July, 1978	Norm Foote and others	Near mouth of Ausable River, N.Y.	–	Water was mirror still	600 ft.
129	July 5, 1977	Sandra and Anthony Mansi	Around St. Albans, VT (Eyewitnesses not sure of exact location)	Around noon to 1 P.M.	Windy, clear with sunshine, wavy lake surface	Approximately 100–150 ft.
130	July, 1977	Liza Bray	Butler Island, VT	3 P.M.	Hot, sultry clear day, absolutely calm lake surface	60–80 ft.
131	August, 1977	Roger and Larry Lorberbaum	Clinton Community College, N.Y.	5 P.M.	Clear, calm lake surface	50–100 yds.
132	Summer 1977	Two VT residents	Carry Bay, VT	–	–	200 yds.
133	June, 1978	Charles and Stephen Mazurowski	1–1½ mi. south of Crown Point bridge	7 P.M.	Water was calm	½ mi. to 1000 yds.

Eyewitness(es)' Description of Champ	Remarks	Information From:
7 ft. long and a foot wide, black in color	Observed from house overlooking North West Bay	*Albany Times-Union* (November 23, 1975)
30 ft. long, animal moved up and down and seemed as though it was eating something	Observed while fishing at mouth of Rock River	From cassette tape by J. Tremblay
Head and neck 3 ft. above water, dark/black in color	–	Completed sighting sheet from Nancy Warren (August 27, 1981)
20 ft. long, head upright with long neck, 2 humps, brownish in color	–	Completed sighting sheet from Orville Wells to Bob Bartholomew (September 18, 1979)
In excess of 10 ft. in length	They thought this could be a sturgeon	Letter from Footes (October 26, 1978)
15–20 ft. long, head and neck 6–8 ft. in height out of water, smooth to semi-smooth skin, black or dark brown in color	Animal photographed by Sandra Mansi	Completed sighting sheets from Sandra and Anthony Mansi (January 1, 1980)
20–30 ft. long, very dark. . .dark gray in color	Observed from a cliff above lake	Completed sighting sheet from Liza Bray (January 1, 1981)
20–30 ft., black in color	–	Completed sighting sheet from Roger Lorberbaum (September 17, 1981)
Snake with small head and 3 humps, neck 3 or 4 ft. long	Observed while fishing from shore	From interview conducted by David Salonin with one of the eyewitnesses on January 9, 1982, and interview written up on January 10, 1982
Horse-shaped head about 1 ft. thick and 2–3 ft. long, hump-like objects behind head	Animal moving 5 m.p.h.	Letter from Mazurowskis (August 6, 1978)

Sighting	Date	Eyewitness(es)	Location	Time	Weather and Lake Surface Conditions	Range
134	June, 1978	Nancy S. Robinson and family	Between Cumberland Head and Valcour Island, N.Y.	A.M. (morning)	Warm and very clear	700–800 ft.
135	June, 1978	Cecile M. Reus	Off Jackson Point, South Hero, VT	–	Clear; sunny; some clouds and very, very calm lake surface	800 ft.
136	August 17, 1978	Mr. and Mrs. James Newell, Carolyn Benn	Essex, N.Y.	5:30 P.M.	Very calm	–
137	August, 1978	Captain Richard M. Dickson	Off the Plattsburgh, N.Y. Air Force Marina	Around 7–8 P.M.	Cloudy, cool, had rained earlier, surface as calm as glass	50 yds.
138	August, 1978	Marge and Melvin Grandjean	Bulwagga Bay, N.Y.	9 A.M.	Sunshine, calm lake surface	125 ft.
139	Summer 1978	Mrs. Colleen Van Hoven and son	South of Essex, N.Y.	4 or 5 P.M.	Lake surface like glass	–
140	September 3, 1978	Alice Mazuzan	Bulwagga Bay, N.Y.	About 4 P.M.	Sunny, calm	–
141	May or June, 1979	Alexander E. Cameron	Rock River and Missisquoi Bay, VT	7:30 P.M.	Rain	20 ft.
142	August 3, 1979	Clark Winslow and several others	Between Valcour Island and Corlear Bay, N.Y.	11:30 P.M.	Big moon	–
143	August 26, 1979	Ben and Dottie Stein	1 mi. west of McNeil Cove, VT	3:30 P.M.	Calm	100–200 yds.

Eyewitness(es)' Description of Champ	Remarks	Information From:
Looked like the old Sinclair dinosaur, 12 ft. long, head 7½ ft. out of water	–	Completed sighting sheet from Nancy S. Robinson (July 6, 1981)
20–30 ft. long; head, neck and 2 humps observed; dark or black in color	–	Letter from Cecile M. Reus (May 20, 1982) and completed sighting sheet from Cecile M. Reus (June 2, 1982)
3 sections each 10 ft. long, serpent-like, dark gray/black in color	–	Letter from Mrs. Newell (October 14, 1978) and letter from Carolyn Benn (November 14, 1978)
3 or 4 low humps, dark brown/black in color	Observed while fishing from a jetty	Completed sighting sheet from Richard M. Dickson (September 17, 1980)
12 ft. long, bony back, part of head out of water, dark in color	–	Completed sighting sheet from the Grandjeans (September 25, 1980)
10–15 ft. of dark area just below water level	They thought they observed Champ "just below the surface"	Letter from Colleen Van Hoven (October 24, 1978)
2 humps, black in color	Observed from restaurant overlooking bay	Completed sighting sheet from Alice Mazuzan (November 8, 1980)
20 ft. visible, looked like an island, green moss in color, rough skin surface	Observer fishing at the time	Completed sighting sheet from Alexander E. Cameron (January 15, 1980)
20–25 ft. long, animate, 1½ ft. high	Observed from a boat	From a phone conversation with Mr. Clark Winslow (July 7, 1981)
3 humps	Observed from sailboat, animal moving at speed of 5–10 knots	Letter from Steins (September 3, 1979), Burlington Free Press (August 28, 1979), and phone interview (August 26, 1979)

Sighting	Date	Eyewitness(es)	Location	Time	Weather and Lake Surface Conditions	Range
144	Summer 1979	Nancy S. Robinson and family	Between Cumberland Head and Valcour Island, N.Y.	A.M. (morning)	Warm and very clear	700–800 ft.
145	September, 1979	Alice Pratt	3 mi. north of Port Henry, N.Y.	–	Clear and calm lake surface	50 ft.
146	Around July 3, 1980	Jan Gove, husband, and son	Off north end of Knight Island, VT	6 P.M.	Very clear, sunny, no wind, fairly calm lake surface	150–200 ft.
147	July 18, 1980	Thomas A. Westphal and family	West of Knight Island, VT	10:30 A.M.	Clear, South wind at 10–15 m.p.h.	300 yds.
148	July, 1980	Mr. and Mrs. Patrick S. Robins and a friend	Off Burlington, VT breakwater	10:30 P.M.	Moonlit night	20 ft.
149	August, 1980	Milo Drake	Port Henry, N.Y.	7:30 P.M.	Clear, calm lake surface	300 ft.
150	Summer 1980	Nancy S. Robinson and family	Between Cumberland Head and Valcour Island, N.Y.	A.M. (morning)	Warm and very clear	700–800 ft.
151	Summer 1980	W. Jay Kohen, Glen Estus	–	Early afternoon	No wind, no waves, absolutely calm	175–250 ft.
152	September 13, 1980	Crystal Cadieux, Craig Mowry	South of Plattsburgh, N.Y.	Approximately 8:30 P.M.	Light rain, very smooth surface	200 ft.
153	October 4, 1980	Howard F. Brown, Helena Hazen	Bow Arrow Point, VT	2 P.M.	Sunny, lake surface smooth as glass	175–200 ft.

Eyewitness(es)' Description of Champ	Remarks	Information From:
Looked like the old Sinclair dinosaur, 12 ft. long, head 7½ ft. out of water	(Details of their sighting same as their June, 1978 sighting)	Completed sighting sheet from Nancy S. Robinson (July 6, 1981)
About 20 ft. long, black in color	–	Completed sighting sheet from Alice Pratt (January 21, 1981)
Approximately 20–30 ft. long, very dark – black in color	Observed while fishing in boat	Letter from Jan Gove (October 8, 1980) and completed sighting sheet from Jan Gove (October 20, 1980)
30 ft. long, snake-like, top of head seen, black in color	Observed from a boat, 3 sightings over a 30 minute span, film footage from Nikon 8:1 Super 8 mm camera shot	Completed sighting sheet from the Westphals (August 15, 1980)
Whale-shaped creature, looked like an upturned boat, smooth-backed, dark or gray in color	Observed from boat while cruising	Letter from Patrick S. Robins (April 10, 1981)
30 ft. long, 2 ft. out of water, 3 big humps, smooth skin, black or dark gray in color	Observed while fishing	Completed sighting sheet from Milo Drake (December 6, 1982)
Looked like the old Sinclair dinosaur, 12 ft. long, head 7½ ft. out of water	(Details of their sighting same as their June, 1978 and Summer, 1979 sightings)	Completed sighting sheet from Nancy S. Robinson (July 6, 1981)
Large, dark sections only 2 ft. long exposed, one foot thick	Animal moved at speed of 5–10 m.p.h.	Letter from W. Jay Kohen (August 12, 1981)
Head/neck about 5 to 6 ft. out of water, off white/darkish green in color	Observed from car off Rt. 9	Completed sighting sheet from Crystal Cadieux and Craig Mowry (September 23, 1980)
Approximately 15–18 ft., 1 ft. fin about middle of back, dark brown or gray in color	–	Completed sighting sheet from Howard F. Brown (October 22, 1980) and completed sighting sheet from Helena Hazen (March 14, 1981)

Sighting	Date	Eyewitness(es)	Location	Time	Weather and Lake Surface Conditions	Range
154	April 7, 1981	Doug Morse, Jr., Tammy Burke	Fort Ticonderoga, N.Y.	6:25 P.M.	Clear, slight wind, calm lake surface	1 mi.
155	April 17, 1981	Barbara Boyle, Camilla K. Rich, Jane Sullivan, Esther Waldron	Bulwagga Bay, N.Y.	10 A.M.	Overcast skies, misty, lake surface was a bit choppy	–
156	April 19, 1981	Robert E. Hughes and family	Port Henry, N.Y.	5:30 P.M.	Cloudy, kind of calm lake surface	¾ mi.
157	April 28, 1981	Albert Jerry, Fred and Cathy Timmerman, and George Bessette	St. Albans Bay, VT	Between 1–2 P.M.	–	–
158	May 24, 1981	W. Jay Kohen, family, and friends	Halfway between Westport, N.Y. and Port Henry, N.Y. (just north of Stevenson Bay)	Around 5 P.M.	Sunny	Varied: 300–400 ft. to 25 ft.
159	June 10, 1981	Marty Santos and friend	Off west shore of Grand Isle, VT	Around 7:30–8 P.M.	Calm	15 ft.
160	June 13, 1981	Norma Manning, Ann Manning, Michael Manning	Port Henry, N.Y.	5:45 P.M.	Sunny, calm lake surface	–
161	June 28, 1981	Janet Sullivan, Carlos Salazar, and Mr. and Mrs. Thomas Sullivan	Potash Bay, VT	8:15–8:30 P.M.	Lake like glass	¼ mi. to 100 yds.

Eyewitness(es)' Description of Champ	Remarks	Information From:
6 ft. of animal's length out of water, 2 black humps	—	Completed sighting sheet from Doug Morse, Jr. and Tammy Burke (April 27, 1981)
30–40 ft., 3 humps, possibly a head, dark, black, or dark brown in color	—	From correspondence with eyewitnesses, *Albany Times-Union* (April 18, 1981), and *Burlington Free Press* (April 20, 1981)
25–30 ft. long, black or dark green in color	Creature just beneath lake surface	Completed sighting sheet from Robert E. Hughes (April 27, 1981)
2½ ft. of neck and head observed, huge, looked something like a horse	—	*Burlington Free Press* (April 30, 1981)
20 ft. long, large hump and jagged back, black in color	First observed from shore by a group and then observed closer up by 4 people from a boat	*Burlington Free Press* (May 25, 1981)
30 ft. long	Observed from boat while fishing, Marty Santos believed Champ was feeding on perch (fish feeding on "an incredible bug hatching"), Champ, according to Santos, may have been attracted to his 8 ft. long boat by the hum of its electric motor	Phone interview with Marty Santos (June 29, 1981) and *New York Times* (June 30, 1981)
10 ft. long, dark brown in color	—	Completed sighting sheet from Norma Manning (July 2, 1981)
25–30 ft. long, 2 humps, smooth skin, light brown in color	Observed from boat while fishing and observed from shore	Completed sighting sheet and letter from Janet Sullivan (January 21 and 22, 1981)

189

Sighting	Date	Eyewitness(es)	Location	Time	Weather and Lake Surface Conditions	Range
162	July 2, 1981	George H. Bunnell, Mr. and Mrs. John J. Marchelewicz	Near Rock Harbor, N.Y.	2:30 P.M.	Sunshine, clear, lake surface was dead glassy calm	150 yds.
163	July 3, 1981	Kelley J. Williams and several others	Bulwagga Bay, N.Y.	–	–	–
164	July 9, 1981	Kelley J. Williams	Bulwagga Bay, N.Y.	Approaching dusk	Calm	75 yds.
165	July 9, 1981	Gerald Williams, Jr.	Port Henry, N.Y.	5:30 P.M.	Sunny but partially cloudy, slight waves	80 ft.
166	July 11, 1981	Norma J. Parah and family	Off west shore of Woods Island, VT	8:50 P.M.	–	1500 ft.
167	July 16, 1981	Mary Carty and several others	Off Shelburne Farms estate, VT	4:30 P.M.	Calm lake surface	½ mi.
168	July 18, 1981	Maurice and Yvette Delorme	Between North Hero Island and Butler Island, VT	4:30 P.M.	Clear, exceptionally calm lake surface	150 ft.
169	August 3, 1981	William James Knight, wife, family, Barbara LaFontaine, and others	Off Adams Landing, Grand Isle, VT	Mid afternoon	A bit cloudy with some mist on lake, calm lake surface	150 yds.
170	August 15, 1981	Gary Michener	Bulwagga Bay, N.Y.	7:05 A.M.	Very clear, lake like a mirror	150 yds.

190

Eyewitness(es)' Description of Champ	Remarks	Information From:
Only observed 5-6 ft. of length, height 2 ft., width 1 ft., ridges on back, neck observed, slimy, dark in color	Observed from a sloop, Champ moved up and down like a dolphin or porpoise	Completed sighting sheet from George H. Bunnell (July 17, 1981)
–	–	Completed sighting sheet from Kelley J. Williams (August 3, 1981)
Over 30 ft. long, head partially out of water, black in color	Observed from shore, photographs taken with Keystone XR 108 camera with 110 film, one photograph appeared in *Life* magazine (August, 1982)	Completed sighting sheet from Kelley J. Williams (August 3, 1981)
Head was 4-5 ft. long; eyes about 6-7 in. in diameter, animal was shiny black, possibly dark gray in color	–	Completed sighting sheet from Gerald Williams, Jr. (October 1, 1981)
3 humps about 2 ft. long and 2 ft. apart, black or dark brown in color	–	Letter from Norma J. Parah (July 15, 1981)
40-60 ft. long, several humps, some eyewitnesses claimed they observed animal's head	Photographed by Mary Carty using a 35 mm camera with telephoto lens – one of Mary Carty's photographs was published in *Life* magazine (August, 1982)	*Burlington Free Press* (July 18, 1981) and phone conversations with Mary Carty (July 17, 1981 and July 28, 1981)
2 large humps 14-16 in. high	–	*The Islander* (July 18, 1981)
40 ft. long, dark (rather black) in color	Several photographs taken with a camera using a 150 mm zoom lens	Letter from William James Knight (October 8, 1981) and completed sighting sheet from William J. Knight (October 7, 1981)
30-40 ft. long, 12-14 humps, dark, possibly black in color	Humps said to be rising and falling as it moved	Completed sighting sheet from Gary Michener (October 21, 1981)

Sighting	Date	Eyewitness(es)	Location	Time	Weather and Lake Surface Conditions	Range
171	August 22, 1981	Mary M. Morgan and friend	Between Valcour Island and South Hero, VT	—	Not much wind	50–200 ft.
172	Mid August, 1981	Molly Ann Fraser and children	Holiday Point, North Hero, VT	4 P.M.	Clear, sunny, water still	100 yds.
173	August, 1981	—	Maquam Road at Sampsons Point, VT	10 A.M.	Warm, glass-like, smooth lake surface	50 ft.
174	August, 1981	Claude Van Kleeck and others	Bulwagga Bay, N.Y.	—	—	50 ft. or less
175	May 1, 1982	Raymond W. Sargent	44° 45.5'N Latitude 73° 23.0'W Longitude (southeast of Long Point, N.Y.)	1:30 P.M.	Sunshine, clear, calm lake surface	150 yds.
176	May 8, 1982	Theresa Whitaker, Nina W. Mandy, and others	Bulwagga Bay, N.Y.	6:10 P.M.	Clear	150 yds.
177	May 27, 1982	Susan Sherman, Carol Anson	Bulwagga Bay, N.Y.	10 A.M.	Hazy, small waves	—
178	May 29, 1982	John and Nina W. Mandy	Bulwagga Bay, N.Y.	8:15 A.M.	—	300 yds.
179	May 30, 1982	James A. and Gerda Carroll	1½ mi. S.E. of the Four Brothers and 4 mi. due west of Shelburne Point, VT	—	Clear, sunshine, lake surface calm as glass	40–50 ft.
180	June 10, 1982	Debbie Towne	Port Henry, N.Y.	Around 4:30–5 P.M.	Clear, sunshine, very calm lake surface	—

Eyewitness(es)' Description of Champ	Remarks	Information From:
A head at front of a wake	Observed while sailing, Mary M. Morgan observed it with binoculars	Letter from Mary M. Morgan (April 17, 1982)
1 non-segmented animal, top of a smooth head observed that looked like that of a seal, dark or black-like in color	–	Completed sighting sheet from Molly Ann Fraser (August 10, 1982)
12–15 ft. long, about 2 ft. out of water, black in color	–	From written sheet completed by eyewitness and provided to me in April, 1982
Not less than 50 ft long, at least as wide as a 55 gallon barrel, swam in an up and down fashion	Observed from a 12 ft. boat, speed of animal said to be no less than 40 m.p.h.	Letter from Claude Van Kleeck (August 31, 1982)
About 18–24 in. of head and neck on surface, about 10–12 in. in diameter	After the animate object submerged and Raymond W. Sargent's boat passed over the sighting area, his "sonar depth sounder became erratic showing a blip at every digit on the scale markings"	Letter from Raymond W. Sargent (May 28, 1982) and completed sighting sheet (June 8, 1982)
20 ft. long, 3 humps, grayish black in color	–	Completed sighting sheet from Theresa Whitaker (May 24, 1982) and letter from Nina W. Mandy (July 23, 1982)
Animal basking in sun, oval shaped head, neck long like a snake, dark or dark green in color	–	Completed sighting sheet from Susan Sherman (December 11, 1982)
3 black humps and the wake behind	–	Letter from Nina W. Mandy (July 23, 1982)
30–50 ft. long, approximately 15 ft. visible to observers, ridges on back, head and neck. 1–2 ft. high, dark brown in color but a light yellowish streak from front of head to below the waterline	Observed from a yacht	Completed sighting sheet from James A. and Gerda Carroll (June 5, 1982)
3 humps, it looked like a giant snake, black or very dark green in color	–	Completed sighting sheet from Debbie Towne (December 6, 1982)

Sighting	Date	Eyewitness(es)	Location	Time	Weather and Lake Surface Conditions	Range
181	July 14, 1982	Margaret Witherbee	West of Valcour Island, N.Y.	–	Clear, sunshine, calm lake surface	110 yds.
182	July 19, 1982	Claude Van Kleeck, Ed Avery, Joyce and Sam Ruggles	Bulwagga Bay, N.Y.	5:30 P.M.	Overcast sky, clear, calm lake surface	100–150 yds.
183	August 1, 1982	John Annette, Michael Dumar	Rouses Point, N.Y.	Dusk	–	–
184	August 5, 1982	Edward Sheldon, Shawn Elvidge, Dan Ormsby	King Bay, N.Y.	7:30 P.M.	No wind, calm lake surface	100 yds.
185	October 6, 1982	About 30 people	Rouses Point, N.Y.	Afternoon	Calm	–
186	October 27, 1982	Linda Effel and daughter	West shore of Grand Isle, VT (Approximately ½ mi. north of fishing access area)	Approximately 11 A.M.	Sunny, windless, lake surface smooth as glass	–
187	Autumn 1982	Mrs. Cathy Cooper	Rouses Point, N.Y.	Morning	It had been raining, lake was calm as it could be	Fairly close to shore
188	Autumn 1982	Two Rouses Point, N.Y. residents	Rouses Point, N.Y.	–	–	–
189	May 3, 1983	Barbara and Theresa Drinkwine, and one other person	Crown Point, N.Y.	–	Overcast	–

Eyewitness(es)' Description of Champ	Remarks	Information From:
Just the body observed	It was travelling approximately 40 m.p.h.	Completed sighting sheet from Margaret Witherbee (December 2, 1982)
45–50 ft. long, 24–30 in. high, 36–40 in. wide, serpent-shaped head, blackish gray in color	Photographed by Claude Van Kleeck, with a Canon AE-1 camera, but film did not advance. Also photographed by Joyce Ruggles, but apparently no definitive image on the film	Completed sighting sheet from Claude Van Kleeck (August 25, 1982), completed sighting sheet from Ed Avery (July 26, 1982), and *Albany Times-Union* (July 25, 1982)
12–20 ft. long, swam more like an eel than a fish, Michael Dumar said they saw a head, it looked like a periscope sticking out of the water	John Annette and Michael Dumar are Rouses Point police officers	*Valley News* (August 18, 1982)
A big black animal, like a huge snake with 3 humps, black in color	Animal said to have hit a 24 or 30 ft. sailboat upon leaving the bay	*Plattsburgh Press Republican* (August 7, 1982)
3 humps	The animal submerged after being buzzed by a seaplane	*The North Countryman* (October 13, 1982)
2 separate long, thick heads showing above surface	Linda Effel convinced she saw 2 Champ animals	Letter from Linda Effel (October 13, 1983)
3 humps, black—a dark color	—	*The North Countryman* (October 6, 1982)
Long and dark, head and tail, dark in color	This sighting was same day as Mrs. Cathy Cooper's sighting, but later in the day	*The North Countryman* (October 6, 1982)
Large object, head	—	Letter from Barbara Drinkwine (June 28, 1983)

Sighting	Date	Eyewitness(es)	Location	Time	Weather and Lake Surface Conditions	Range
190	Memorial Day Weekend, 1983	Jane and Harry Atkinson	Between Burton Island, VT and Sandbar causeway	–	Overcast	250 yds.
191	June 5, 1983	Raymond Tolar and a neighboring camper	Near Macomb Bay, VT	7 P.M.	After a long day of rain	–
192	June 13, 1983	Beverly Fraser	Near Chazy Landing, N.Y.	7:30 P.M.	Clear, water was like glass	30–35 ft.
193	June 14, 1983	Dick L. Noel, Tim L. Noel	North Hero, VT	7:10– 7:17 P.M.	Clear, but hazy, very calm surface	550 ft.
194	June 15, 1983	Suzanne Starr, Greg Wildasin, and several others	Fort Cassin, VT (mouth of Otter Creek)	7 A.M.	Clear, slightly hazy, perfectly calm lake surface	65–85 yds.
195	June 16, 1983	Robert and Kevin Alger	Cumberland Head, N.Y.– Near lighthouse	3 P.M.	Clear, sunshine	75 ft.
196	June 19, 1983	Joe and Toni Krupka	.1–.2 mi. N.E. of Peru Dock, south of Plattsburgh, N.Y.	8:30– 8:40 P.M.	Clear, glass-like, very smooth lake surface	.1–.2 mi.
197	June 21, 1983	Jane Rowe and husband	Beyond the Burlington, VT breakwater	6:15 P.M.	90°F, very calm lake surface	–
198	July 2, 1983	Edie and Philip Jordan	Old railroad causeway, southern point of land, North Hero, VT	7:30 P.M.	–	–
199	July 2, 1983	Ronald S. Kermani, Susan Kopp	About 1 mi. north of Crown Point Boat Launch (slip)	8 P.M.	No wind, as calm as glass	200 yds.

Eyewitness(es)' Description of Champ	Remarks	Information From:
Only about 4 ft. in length out of water and 1 ft. in diameter at base, slightly curved	Observed from a boat	Letter from Harry Atkinson (no date on letter)
A rounded object thought to be a head at the front of a wake, dark in color	Object travelling approximately 5 m.p.h.	Letter from Raymond Tolar (November 1, 1983)
10–15 ft. long, a dark shadow	2 were present underwater, swimming at a rate of around 3 m.p.h.	Completed sighting sheet from Beverly Fraser (June 20, 1983)
20–25 ft. long, height 3–4 ft., long neck and 2 or 3 humps, dark or black in color	The Noels thought it was undulating through the water	Completed sighting sheet from Dick L. Noel and Tim L. Noel (June 27, 1983)
30–40 ft. long, 4 humps (each 6–8 ft. long and 1 ft. high), dark or dark gray to black in color	Suzanne Starr thought it could have been 1 large creature or 4 smaller ones	Completed sighting sheet from Suzanne Starr (June 24, 1983) and Greg Wildasin (June 25, 1983)
Just under the surface, like a back fin breaking water	Robert Alger believes he saw two creatures—one behind the other	Completed sighting sheet from Robert Alger (June 30, 1983)
20–30 ft. long, 10–12 in. wide, 3–4 black ridges	–	Completed sighting sheet from Joe Krupka (June 23, 1983)
3 parts, very dark in color	–	Letter to Anne K. Baker, of Lake Champlain Committee, from Jane Rowe (June 22, 1983)
30–40 ft. long, large black humps	Observed while photographing old railroad causeway, photographs taken, but nothing significant shown	Letter from Philip Jordan (August 18, 1983) and phone interview (July 10, 1983)
2 humps, 1.5–2 ft. height out of water, humps undulated, moved 1–2 m.p.h., dark in color	Observed while fishing from a rowboat	Completed sighting sheet from Ronald S. Kermani (August 27, 1983) and Albany Times-Union (August 14, 1983)

197

Sighting	Date	Eyewitness(es)	Location	Time	Weather and Lake Surface Conditions	Range
200	July 7, 1983	About 35 people	Camp Grey-lock, South Hero, VT	2:45 P.M.	–	35 ft. from camp dock
201	July 14, 1983	Mrs. Jane Marsh, Mrs. Kimball Prince	South of Willsboro, N.Y.	7 A.M.	Absolutely flat lake surface	About 150 ft.
202	July 17, 1983	Mrs. Betty Hebert and family	Rouses Point, N.Y.	Be-tween 11–11:30 A.M.	Lake fairly calm	100 ft.
203	July 17, 1983	Steven and Norma Deforge and two sons	Off East Shore Road near Camp Marycrest, Grand Isle, VT	6:45 P.M.	Calm bay	200 ft.
204	August 6, 1983	Beatrice M. Jochum and mother	Near Hospital Creek, VT	2:15 P.M.	Clear, sunshine, calm lake surface	100 yds.
205	August 10, 1983	Mr. E. James Swinyer, M.D., Avis Swinyer, Irene Domina	St. Albans Bay, VT vicinity	7:30 P.M.	No wind, no waves	200 ft.
206	August 12, 1983	Mr. E. James Swinyer, M.D., Avis Swinyer	St. Albans Bay, VT vicinity	7:30 P.M.	Perfectly calm	1000 ft.
207	August 14, 1983	John W. Herbert and family	1 mi. north of Isle La Motte, VT	–	Absolutely flat mirror-like calm	1 mi.
208	August 16, 1983	Richard Alther and 13 other people	Fort Cassin Point, VT	About 7:45 P.M. or later	Absolutely calm lake surface	100 ft.

Eyewitness(es)' Description of Champ	Remarks	Information From:
50 ft. long, 2 brown humps about 6 in. out of water	–	*Plattsburgh Press Republican* (July 11, 1983), *The North Countryman* (July 13, 1983), and *The County Courier* (July 14, 1983)
20 ft. long, 6 humps	They believe they saw 2 monsters, observed with binoculars	Letter to Anne K. Baker of Lake Champlain Committee, from Mrs. Jane Marsh and Mrs. Kimball Prince (July 14, 1983)
10 ft. long or longer, 2 black humps	–	*Plattsburgh Press Republican* (July 19, 1983) and *The North Countryman* (July 20, 1983)
30 ft. in length, head about 1 ft. out of water and the head like one of those plant-eating dinosaurs	Observed while driving	*The Islander* (July 19, 1983)
About 40 ft. long, a head, 3 humps, tail, black in color	Observed in shallow water from their house	Completed sighting sheet from Beatrice M. Jochum (October 9, 1983)
2–3 large dark humps	–	Letter from Mr. E. James Swinyer, M.D. (August 24, 1983)
2 wakes	Dr. Swinyer felt there may have been 2 Champ animals	Letter from Mr. E. James Swinyer, M.D. (August 24, 1983)
Looked like a submarine moving through the water with deck awash, black in color	Observed with 10×50 binoculars and 15× telescope, 1 person observed a head on object	Completed sighting sheet from John W. Herbert (September 28, 1983)
40–50 ft. long, 3 ft. height out of water, black in color	At first 1 wake, then it split into 2 wakes, likely 2 creatures	Completed sighting sheet from Richard Alther (September 1, 1983)

Sighting	Date	Eyewitness(es)	Location	Time	Weather and Lake Surface Conditions	Range
209	August 18, 1983	Several people	Fort Cassin Point, VT	7:30 P.M.	–	–
210	August 23, 1983	Kelly and Brande Pratt and several others	Port Henry, N.Y.	7 P.M.	Sunny, 82°F, lake surface calm with some ripples	–
211	August 27, 1983	Graham Reynolds and two others	Off east shore of Alburg, VT	–	–	–
212	August 27, 1983	Mrs. Eva Gauvin and a friend	Camp Mary-crest, Grand Isle, VT	6:30 P.M.	–	300 yds.
213	–	Tommy Heinrich	–	–	–	–
214	–	Hank Gilbo	Opposite Elm Tree Point going north towards Button Bay, VT	5 or 6 P.M.	Water was very calm	50–60 yds.
215	–	Hank Gilbo	Near Crown Point bridge	–	Windy (10–12 knot wind)	150 yds.
216	–	Hank Gilbo	Bulwagga Bay, N.Y.	–	Calm lake surface	–
217	–	Mrs. Claire Salaway	½ mi. south of Crown Point bridge	–	–	–

Eyewitness(es)' Description of Champ	Remarks	Information From:
Wake, humps, head	–	Completed sighting sheet from Richard Alther (September 1, 1983)
Bubbles, then 2 humps appeared	–	Letter from Kelly and Brande Pratt (November 18, 1983)
30–40 ft. long, 4 humps	–	*The Islander* (September 6, 1983)
20–25 ft. long, 2 humps, and a small head and long neck	Mrs. Eva Gauvin saw it submerge and, shortly there-after, a second view occurred 100 yds. away – possibly a second Champ	Letter from Mrs. Eva Gauvin (September 10, 1983)
20–45 ft. long, head shaped like a horse's head, a long snouted face, eyes visible, two small horns sprouting from creature's forehead, gray or rust-colored	Observed while flycasting from a boat	*Ithaca Journal* (February 15, 1971) and *Monsters Among Us: Journey to the Unexplained* by John Lee and Barbara Moore
Looked like the back of a big whale, gray or greenish color	Observed from a boat	Letter from Hank Gilbo (December 12, 1976)
20 or 25 ft. long	Observed from boat, creature swimming fast against the wind	Letter from Hank Gilbo (December 12, 1976)
Saw snout or what looked "like a snout brownish color sticking about a foot out of water"	Observed from boat, heard sound or noise like a gur-gling sound, 8 mm film footage taken – inconclusive film footage	Letter from Hank Gilbo (December 12, 1976)
A long thing and larger than a boat	Mrs. Claire Salaway heard a strange sound during her sighting that may be from Champ	Letter from Mrs. Claire Salaway (October 7, 1980)

Sighting	Date	Eyewitness(es)	Location	Time	Weather and Lake Surface Conditions	Range
218	–	Barbara Holden and cousin	Burlington, VT	–	–	–
219	–	Bess Sherlock and husband	Port Henry, N.Y.	Early evening	Clear, calm	500 ft.
220	Summer Year ?	Edithe C. Bradshaw	Otter Creek, VT	–	Clear, sunshine	40–60 ft.
221	–	Eugene Viens, Jr. and two other people	From Lookout Rock– Burlington, VT	–	–	–

Late entries

Sighting	Date	Eyewitness(es)	Location	Time	Weather and Lake Surface Conditions	Range
222	September, 1983	Michelle Baker and two other people	Port Henry Beach, Port Henry, NY	Around 7:30 P.M.	Calm lake surface, very humid and warm	about 100 yards

Eyewitness(es)' Description of Champ	Remarks	Information From:
—	Observed when the two were children, from a Burlington, VT park as other people watched, too	Letter from Barbara Holden (1980)
Like a snake, rather dark gray in color	Observed while fishing	Letter from Bess Sherlock (July 26, 1980)
20–30 ft. long, like a huge snake, head like a snake, greenish gray in color with a whitish gray stomach	Observed when Edithe C. Bradshaw was a young girl	Completed sighting sheet from Edithe C. Bradshaw (February 8, 1981)
30 ft. in length, 4 high spots, one of which appeared to be a head	Observed from shore, Champ moved 7–10 m.p.h.	"Does Champ Exist?" Seminar Proceedings (August 29, 1981)
About 25-35 ft. long, dark green or black in color, no head or tail visible, several humps	The animal was distinctly swimming against the current, no boats on the water. First appeared as small waves then rose above the surface and was in view for about 10 or 15 seconds, then gradually lowered its body into the water again	Completed sighting sheet from Michelle Baker (June 14, 1984)

Sighting	Date	Eyewitness(es)	Location	Time	Weather and Lake Surface Conditions	Range
223 & 224	May 21, 1984 May 23, 1984	Anna Gagne Anna & Gabriel Gagne	Off Popasquash Island, between island and shore	5:00 P.M.	Rain, calm lake surface	Approx. 1/8 mi.

Eyewitness(es)' Description of Champ	Remarks	Information From:
Dark brown to black in color. Large, round body out of the water, with a head moving back and forth. Head was 4½–5 feet above surface of lake. Possible fins, or flippers	First day sighted by Anna alone. Second sighting by Anna and Gabriel. They were attracted to the sighting by a noise made by the animal. Gabriel stated the possible fins made it resemble a "large, large bird with its wings tucked back." He went on to say "I don't care what anybody else says now, I know it's there!"	Telephone conversation with Gabriel Gagne, May 23, 1984, from a lead by Stuart Hall of WCAX-TV, Burlington, VT.

Fishes Of The Lake Champlain Basin*

From: Lake Champlain Planning Guide: For Water And Related Land Resources, June, 1976 (Sponsored by: State of New York, State of Vermont, and The New England River Basins Commission)

Family	Common Name	Family	Common Name
Lampreys	Sea Lamprey		Pearl Dace
	Silver Lamprey		Northern Redbelley Dace
	Brook Lamprey		Southern Redbelley Dace
Sturgeon	Lake Sturgeon		Blacknose Dace
Gar	Longnose Gar		Finescale Dace
Bowfin	Bowfin		Longnose Dace
Mooneye	Mooneye		Cutlips Minnow
Trouts	Cisco (Lake Herring)		Brassy Shiner
	Lake Whitefish		Silvery Minnow
	Round Whitefish		Golden Shiner
	Lake Trout		Emerald Shiner
	Brown Trout		Bridle Shiner
	Brook Trout		Striped Shiner
	Rainbow Trout		Blackchin Shiner
	Atlantic Salmon		Blacknose Shiner
			Spottail Shiner
Smelts	Rainbow Smelt		Sand Shiner
			Mimic Shiner
Mudminnow	Central Mudminnow		Fathead Minnow
Pikes	Grass Pickerel		Fallfish
	Chain Pickerel		Common Shiner
	Northern Pike		Rosyface Shiner
	Muskellunge		Bluntnose Minnow
Minnows and Carp	Carp		Creek Chub
	Goldfish		Lake Chub

Fishes of the Lake Champlain Basin

Family	Common Name	Family	Common Name
Suckers	Quillback		Bluegill
	White Sucker		Smallmouth Bass
	Longnose Sucker		Largemouth Bass
	Silver Redhorse		Black Crappie
	River Carpsucker	Perches	Yellow Perch
	Black Redhorse		Logperch
	Shorthead Redhorse		Sauger
	Greater Redhorse		Walleye
			Eastern Sand Darter
Freshwater	Brown Bullhead		Iowa Darter
Catfishes	Yellow Bullhead		Fantail Darter
	Channel Catfish		Tessellated Darter
	Stonecat		Channel Darter
Freshwater Eel	American Eel	Drum	Freshwater Drum
Codfishes	Burbot	Sculpins	Mottled Sculpin
Trout-Perches	Trout Perch		Slimy Sculpin
		Killifishes	Banded Killifish
Sunfishes	Rock Bass		
	Pumpkin Seed	Sticklebacks	Brook Stickelback

* All of the Lake Champlain Basin is included, as fish in the tributaries occasionally reach the Lake proper, and, therefore, must be included in any list of Lake Champlain fishes.

Source: William D. Countryman, "Checklist of the Recent Fishes of Vermont" (October, 1975).
Vermont Department of Fish & Game, Agency of Environmental Conservation.

Update

Appendix 6 was added to this second edition of CHAMP—BEYOND THE LEGEND to update readers on the story of Lake Champlain's mystery animals since the first edition of the book was published in the Summer, 1984. The first of the two sections of this appendix—"Recently Recorded Sightings Of Champ"—will chronicle sightings of Champ not printed in Appendix 4. I have tried to provide as many details of these Champ sightings as possible, but at times have been restricted by limited details provided by the eyewitness(es). Appendix 4 lists 224 Champ sightings, so I have started this list at #225.

The second part of this appendix, "1984-1987 Champ-related Field Work Update," documents the Champ field investigations from 1984-1987.

Recently Recorded Sightings Of Champ

(#225) 1880: "The Lake Champlain sea-serpent was seen again, just before the lake closed over, by a party of gentlemen from Shelburn (Shelburne) and Hinesburg. It was in Shelburn (Shelburne) bay (Bay), rose 12 feet out of the water, appeared to be two feet thick, and was covered with scales which glistened like the precious metals in the sun." (*Express & Standard*, Newport, VT, February 24, 1880)

(#226) September 26, 1886: Mr. Root and Mr. Benson; "the famous serpent" described as a hundred ft. long and shaped like a porpoise; sighting from Bouquet House, NY; range 200 ft.; sighting at 4 P.M. (*Plattsburgh Morning Telegram*, September 27, 1886)

(#227) July 14, 1929: Thomas Bridge, David Riley, and Wesley Quimbly; mouth of Bouquet River, NY; while the trio was fishing they observed the Sea Serpent or huge fish (*Ticonderoga Sentinel*, July 18, 1929)

Update

(**#228**) July, 1946: Marilyn Dickovick and husband; Alburg, VT; while out fishing in a rowboat the couple saw Champ described as 3 large coils, 8–10 in. diameter; 15–20 ft. long; dark brown in color; smooth lake surface; sunny; range 15–20 ft.; sighting before 5 P.M. (Completed sighting sheet from Marilyn Dickovick, July 28, 1987)

(**#229**) Summer, 1947: Leo Duval; off Crown Point, NY bridge; saw what looked like a huge black snake approximately 20 ft. long and approximately 8 in. thick; it moved in undulating fashion (Letter to Jane Sullivan from Leo Duval, April 21, 1981)

(**#230**) July 2 or 3, 1950: Marilyn G. Agosta and husband; Port Kent, NY; "We both saw a very large 'creature' . . ."; range within 200 ft.; evening, but a moonlight night (Letter from Marilyn G. Agosta, September 5, 1986)

(**#231**) Circa 1960: Lauri Aixen and mother; Samson's Point, VT; observed from their camp; "It had a small head and seemed to have 3 humps behind it. Mom told me she thought it was a 'sea monster',," said Lauri Aixen (Letter from Lauri Aixen, July 31, 1986)

(**#232**) Circa 1960: Lauri Aixen; while with her brother and in boat going to Butler's Is., VT; she said, "I saw something under the boat it was like a large fish but it went on and on. It had a top fin and moved fast without upsetting the boat . . ." (Letter from Lauri Aixen, July 31, 1986)

(**#233**) August, 1961: Mrs. John B. Burns Jr. and 6 other campers; Colchester Point, VT; saw something that was twice the size of a man swimming; range 150 yds.; sighting at 7:15 P.M. (*Burlington Free Press*, August 30, 1961)

(**#234**) 1966 or 1967: Viola Graves and husband; Owls Head, VT; ". . . we saw in the middle of the lake, what we thought was a log breaking water – but – we watched and then part of it disappeared, and we kept on watching, then saw what could have been the head of ? as it was up out of the water a bit and looked 'rough' or points of some kind – and it was heading north on the Lake – we then spoke of it and realized it was not a log, but could have been – the Loch Monster that we heard talk of –"; very calm lake; sighting in early evening (Letter from Viola Graves, May 21, 1986)

(**#235**) August, 1970: Dr. Eugene Lepeschkin & wife; while boarding the Plattsburgh ferry (NY side) they saw Champ; "I thought it was a horse or moose swimming, but also thought of Champ since I had just read the story in *Vermont Life*. As soon as I could get out of the car I went to the railing, but there was no trace of the head. Either it was Champ or the horse had drowned," wrote Lepeschkin; range 200 yds.; sighting about 8 P.M. (Completed sighting sheet from Dr. Eugene Lepeschkin, February 8, 1986)

(**#236**) August, 1970: William H. Lloyd Jr.; approx. 2 mi. south of Willsboro Point, NY; while boating Lloyd saw Champ-like animal; at time eyewitness had never heard of Champ and thought his sighting was possibly of "an otter or mink or beaver"; very calm lake surface; sunny; range 50–75 yds.; sighting lasted 15–20 min.; sighting at 12 noon (Completed sighting sheet from William H. Lloyd Jr., August 10, 1986)

(#237) Late Summer or early Autumn, 1979: Jackie Allen and friend; no location provided; for about 3 min. they saw Champ's head/neck/back (Letter from Jackie Allen, September 6, 1986)

(#238) 1979: Dennis and Janet Hall; "Orville's Marsh," Ferrisburg, VT; they heard a series of 4 loud splashes then saw a pair of red eyes; range 50 ft. (*Burlington Free Press*, August 12, 1985)

(#239) June 27, 1981: Judy Liner and Larry O'Brien; Malletts Bay, VT; while boating the pair saw Champ; Judy Liner described it as "this dark bumpy thing just floating there"; range 300 yds. (*Burlington Free Press*, July 1, 1981)

(#240) August 8, 1981: Scott Davis and Weston Naef; between Stevenson Bay, NY and Potash Bay, VT; observed 6 hump-like ridges about 20 ft. long, 4 ft. high, and 4 ft. wide; very calm lake surface; cloudy; range 2 mi.; sighting at 8 A.M. (Completed sighting sheet from Scott Davis and Weston Naef, September 7, 1982; not mailed until August 20, 1984)

(#241) Late June, 1982: Andrew S. Paine and 5 other people; Green Bay—2 bays north of mouth of Bouquet River, NY; 3 humps, 10–15 ft. long and 1–2 ft. wide; greyish in color; almost mirror calm lake surface; overcast; range 50–200 yds.; sighting lasted 15 min. and was about 4:30–5:00 P.M. (Completed sighting sheet from Andrew S. Paine, August 27, 1985)

(#242) Last week of July, 1982: Edward M. Breen, Mr. & Mrs. Andrew S. Breen, Mr. & Mrs. Ken Godfrey, Andrea & Kelly Breen; Plattsburgh, NY toward Crab Is.; 3 humps, possibly 1 hump its neck; dark, almost black in color; 1–1½ ft. in height; calm lake surface; range 150 ft.; sighting about 7 P.M. (Completed sighting sheet from Edward M. Breen, October 25, 1985)

(#243) July 7, 1983: Karen Brinckmann; Willisboro Bay, NY; she saw a wake of water and then for about 3 or 4 sec. saw a large light gray colored object come up approximately 18 in. then submerge; calm lake surface; sunny; range 100 yds.; sighting between 11:30 A.M. and 1 P.M. (Completed sighting sheet from Karen Brinckmann, May 18, 1984)

(#244) October, 1983: Lillian Cayo and other people; Champ observed travelling from Lapans Bay area toward Burton's Is., VT; very warm with calm waters; sighting between 7 and 7:30 P.M. (Letter from Lillian Cayo, August 3, 1985)

(#245) 1983: David Jerome; Panton, VT; while Jerome was fishing he saw Champ; Champ 20 ft. long and greenish-brown in color (*Burlington Free Press*, August 12, 1985)

(#246) April, 1984: Roland Haight; between Crown Point, NY and Ticonderoga, NY; while driving from Ticonderoga to Crown Point, Haight said he "saw this large thing moving south in the lake at a moderate speed. I stopped my car . . . When I got out the object had disappeared . . . I judge the animal had considerable size to produce the size wake it did."; lake surface smooth; sighting between 1 and 2 P.M. (Completed sighting sheet from Roland Haight, August 15, 1985)

(#247) May 23, 1984: Lillian and Herbert Cayo; off Lapans Point, VT in direction of Burton's Is., VT; Champ observed for 10 min.; 30 ft. long and greenish brown – very dark in color; calm lake surface; range 200 yds.; sighting at 4 P.M. (Letters from Lillian Cayo, May 27, 1985 and August 3, 1985; completed sighting sheet from Lillian Cayo, June 9, 1985)

(#248) July 5, 1984: Ronald C. Daly and Matt Cronin; Shelburne Bay, VT; head and 3 humps; animal dark brown or black in color; smooth lake surface; had just stopped raining before sighting; warm weather; range 250–400 yds.; sighting at 5:35 P.M. (Completed sighting sheet from Ronald C. Daly, July 15, 1984)

(#249) July 8, 1984: Jody Benway, Cindy Benway, and several others; near St. Albans, VT; several ripples they thought from a Champ; a photograph was taken with a "small snapshot camera"; photograph inconclusive due to great distance; calm, glass-like lake surface; sighting between 5:30 and 7 P.M. (Letter from Jody Benway, May 29, 1985)

(#250) July 12, 1984: Albert C. Spaulding; 7/10 mi. north of Grand Isle/Cumberland Head Ferry on Grand Isle, VT side; Spaulding observed black swan-like neck with a bulbous head, not a wildfowl; lake surface calm; range 200–300 yds.; sighting at 10:30 A.M. (Letter from Albert C. Spaulding, July 15, 1984)

(#251) July 18, 1984: Janet Hansen and two friends; Bulwagga Bay, Port Henry, NY; while canoeing they saw its "head and long neck in one smooth majestic arch"; seen during a calm before a storm; smooth lake surface; sighting at 6 P.M. (Completed sighting sheet from Janet Hansen, July 19, 1984)

(#252) July 21, 1984: Norma J. Oppenlander and husband; off Shelburne Farms Mansion, Shelburne, VT; while boating the pair saw Champ; brownish green in color and it was undulating; very calm lake surface; range 80–100 ft.; sighting at 1:30 P.M. (Postcard from Norma J. Oppenlander, September 1, 1984)

(#253) July 27 or August 3, 1984: Eric Mills; Ferrisburg, VT; saw a 30 ft. long Champ; observed for 10–15 min. in early afternoon (Letter from Dorothy Mills, August 6, 1984)

(#254) July 28, 1984: William Togueville; Rouses Point, NY; observed 2 Champs – 6 humps on front one (front hump could have been head) and 5 humps on rear Champ; 40–45 ft. long; black in color; relatively calm lake surface; range 800 meters; sighting between 12 noon and 1 P.M. (Completed sighting sheet from William Togueville, August 6, 1984)

(#255) July 28, 1984: Michael Shea, Bette Morris, and approximately 60 other people; aboard cruise vessel *THE SPIRIT OF ETHAN ALLEN* off Appletree Point, VT; Shea said there were 3–5 humps; Morris wrote she saw a head and 3 humps; Champ seen twice; animal about 30 ft. long and dark, gray or brown in color; newspaper accounts at time said photograph(s) taken, but Morris wrote in December, 1984 that she, "Cannot find any pictures taken by anyone on our trip."; range 200 ft.; sightings between 6:30 and 7 P.M. (Various newspaper accounts; July 30, 1984 phone interview with Michael Shea; letters from Bette Morris)

(**#256**) August 2, 1984: Elinor Enever and 2 sons; Rouses Point, NY; they sighted 2 Champs – one (Mother?) 24 ft. long and other (baby?) 12 ft. long; possibly a third Champ shaped like a "log" observed; calm lake surface; sighting at 1:05 P.M. (Letter from Elinor Enever, October 26, 1984)

(**#257**) August 4, 1984: Eric Mills and 2 sisters; "between Gardiner's Island and the small island near shore at Long Point"; while boating observed 1 large hump – grayish green (Letter from Dorothy Mills, August 6, 1984)

(**#258**) August 14, 1984: Jim Thurston, Jr. and several others; Webb estate, Shelburne Point, VT toward Rock Dunder; it was 15 ft. long with 4 humps; brownish fish color and white underneath; it was going about 5 m.p.h.; observed using binoculars; beautiful day; range 100–150 yds.; sighting lasted 5–8 min. at 11:10 A.M. (Phone interview with Jim Thurston, Jr., August 14, 1984)

(**#259**) August 17, 1984: Lillian Cayo and 2 other people; off southwest end of Woods Is. travelling north toward Maquam shores, VT; Champ sighted; hazy weather; sighting lasted about 8 min. at 6:20 P.M. (Letter from Lillian Cayo, August 3, 1985)

(**#260**) May 6, 1985: Alice and Al Brooks; Battery Park, Burlington, VT; it "looked like a long telephone pole propelled through the water with mild wake behind it"; Champ 15–20 ft. long; flat calm lake surface; sighting at 8:20 P.M. (Completed sighting sheet from Alice and Al Brooks, July 11, 1985)

(**#261**) May 22, 1985: Lillian Cayo and 3 others; off Lapans Bay, VT; saw Champ using binoculars; sighting from 5:41–5:48 P.M. (Letter from Lillian Cayo, May 27, 1985)

(**#262**) June 25, 1985: Dennis Hall; observed from Radisson Hotel, Burlington, VT – between Rock Dunder and Juniper Is.; one 15 ft. long hump, then a second hump appeared which Hall believes was another Champ; range 500–600 yds.; sighting at 7:30 P.M. (Phone interview with Dennis Hall, July 1, 1985)

(**#263**) June 29, 1985: Peg McGeoch and Jane Temple; off Scotch Bonnet, near Basin Harbor, VT; Champ "well over 30 feet" long; head/neck similar to a brontosaurus, with head held "about 5 feet above surface"; snakelike body; dark in color; undulated "similar to movement of caterpillar"; calm lake surface, but overcast; range 200 yds.; sighting about 4 P.M. (Completed sighting sheets from Jane Temple and Peg McGeoch, July 6, 1985)

(**#264**) June 30, 1985: Dennis Hall and daughter; Mile Point, VT; Hall shot approximately 20 sec. of Beta videotape of what he claimed was Champ; saw animal's head/neck and Dennis Hall estimated Champ's size at 30 ft.; videotape inconclusive due to 5,000 ft. range (*Burlington Free Press*, August 12, 1985 and personal interviews with Dennis Hall)

Update

(#265) July 1, 1985: Pete Horton; Potash Bay, VT; Horton saw an "unidentified submerged object" with "three, rounded black humps which were proceeding smoothly parallel to the shore"; length 20–30 ft.; perfectly calm lake surface; range 150 yds.; sighting at 8:30 P.M. (Completed sighting sheet from Pete Horton, July 9, 1985)

(#266) July 2, 1985: Ann Koch and Rita Shaffer; Elm Point, near Potash Bay, VT; a 10 ft. long segment of Champ; no head seen; Koch claimed it was "not a fish, not an eel, not a snake"; darkish in color; lake surface fairly calm – ripples; overcast; range 35–45 ft.; sighting at 12 noon (Completed sighting sheet from Ann Koch, July 19, 1985)

(#267) July 20, 1985: F. William Billado, Jr., Gerald C. Milot, and Theodore Kessler; near southern tip of Willsboro Bay, NY; while boating they saw 2 humps exposed that totalled 3 or 4 ft., but they estimated animal's length at 15–20 ft.; range 12–15 ft.; sighting at 11 P.M. (Phone interview with F. William Billado, Jr. on August 23, 1985 and completed sighting sheet from F. William Billado, Jr., October 13, 1985)

(#268) August 5, 1985: Jody Kompanek, husband, and son; west of Meach Cove, VT; ". . . it looked like a huge snake moving through the water in an up and down motion . . . We saw the head . . ."; it was 25 ft. long; black in color; calm lake surface; clear, no wind; range 30–50 yds.; observed while they were boating at 7:30 P.M. (Completed sighting sheet from Jody Kompanek, August 20, 1985)

(#269) August 8, 1985: Jean and Becky Joppru; Mullen Bay, NY; while canoeing they saw 4 or 5 black humps protruding 2 or 3 ft. from water; 30 ft. total length; very calm lake surface; warm; range 60 ft.; sighting 6:15–6:30 P.M. (Completed sighting sheet from Jean Joppru, August 17, 1985)

(#270) August 9, 1985: Becky Joppru; south of Mullen Bay, NY; while canoeing Joppru saw creature similar to August 8, 1985 sighting but 35 ft. long; very calm lake surface; hot, humid, no wind; range ½ mi.; sighting at 12 noon–12:30 P.M. (Completed sighting sheet from Becky Joppru, August 20, 1985)

(#271) August 19, 1985: Wynfred Leary and daughter; North Hero, VT (near Mother's Restaurant); "4 or 5 humps black and shiny and round like a rubber tube going about 5 miles per hr"; 25 ft. total length; sighting at 7:45 P.M. (Letter from Wynfred Leary, September 13, 1985)

(#272) August 20, 1985: Sally Coppersfield and 2 children; Adams Landing, VT; they saw 2 dark humps, each 3 ft. long and 2 ft. out of water; humps appeared to have fins on them; calm lake surface; humps 100 ft. from shore; sighting lasted 10–15 sec. at 5:15 P.M. (*The Islander*, August 27, 1985)

(#273) September 2, 1985: June and Geoffrey Barker; about 100 yds. north of Salmon River, near Valcour Island, NY; Barker took photographs of a wave phenomenon that might be from Champ, but he admits the photographs are not helpful; sighting from his boat; one photograph appeared in September 11, 1985 *Plattsburgh Press Republican*; calm lake surface; partly cloudy; 80–150 yds.

range; sighting at 7:15 P.M. (Completed sighting sheet from Geoffrey Barker, September 10, 1985)

(#274) April 11, 1986: Allen Matton and Greg Thacker; Plattsburgh Bay, NY; saw Champ's neck 4 ft. out of water; neck width 6–8 in.; animal's color dark; Matton said it "looked like a dinosaur you would see in a book or T.V."; near glass-smooth lake surface; range 300–400 yds.; sighting at 6 P.M. (Completed sighting sheet from Allen Matton, May 4, 1986)

(#275) May 27, 1986: Christine Hebert; mouth of Winooski River, north of Burlington, VT; barking dog awakened Hebert at 3 A.M. and she saw an animal swimming by her boat ramp as it was illuminated by an outside lamp; reminded her of a "dinosaur"; green in color and muddy; observed a Champ animal 2 more times that evening as barking dog awakened Hebert each time (Completed sighting sheet from Christine Hebert, July 13, 1986)

(#276) June 2, 1986: Scott Gifford and mother; east shore of Willsboro Point, NY toward Four Brothers Islands; while boating they saw animal that "looked about 30 feet long"; grey-brown in color; lake calm as glass; range 150 ft.; sighting at 8:34 P.M. (Letter from Scott Gifford, August 12, 1986)

(#277) June 3, 1986: Barbara Fortune; Clay Point area, Colchester shore, VT; "3 to 4 dark humps undulating"; little wind and sparkling sun; sighting at 5 or 5:10 P.M. (Letter from Barbara Fortune, June 5, 1986, mailed January 9, 1987)

(#278) June 16, 1986: Mrs. William Kennedy, Mrs. Dorothy Hagood, and Mrs. Thomas Mathers; Basin Harbor, VT; Mrs. Kennedy wrote, "it looked like a dark rounded object moving along at the front of the wake . . . there was a slight hump part way back. There were no boats in the water, or was there any person swimming."; lake "like a sea of glass"; animal 50 yds. offshore; sighting at 7:30 P.M. (Letter from Mrs. William Kennedy, September 11, 1986)

(#279) July 1, 1986: Christine Hebert and mother; same location as May 27, 1986 sighting; animal observed at night; barking dog awakened Hebert and her mother; same description of animal as May 27, 1986 sighting; range 50 ft.; observed for 10 min. (Completed sighting sheet from Christine Hebert, July 13, 1986)

(#280) July 4, 1986; Lee Tucker, wife, wife's sister, and wife's father; Willsboro Bay, NY; 2 humps observed offshore; notches on humps; animal dark brown, almost black in color; Tucker used binoculars; Tucker did not think he observed 1 or several sturgeon; sighting about 2:30–3 P.M. (Phone interview with Lee Tucker, July 14, 1986)

(#281) July 6, 1986: John Holt-Harris III, mother, and father; Buoy 39 Marina, Orwell, VT; animal 20 ft. long; back hump observed; animal grayish in color; lake surface like glass; blue sky; range about 50 yds.; sighting at 10:30 A.M. (Completed sighting sheet from John Holt-Harris III, July 30, 1986)

(#282) July 7, 1986: Al Trost; north of Essex, NY; while walking dog along lake, Trost saw an unidentified swimming object at a range of 1,000 ft. on quiet waters;

Update

animal moved at a speed of up to 10–15 m.p.h.; sighting lasted 30 min. at 7:30 P.M. (*The Valley News*, July 16, 1986)

(**#283**) July 16, 1986: Mrs. Kimball Prince and Anne P. Marsh; near Point Elizabeth, Willsboro, NY; saw a 15 ft. long, dark hump; observed it using binoculars; sighting at 6:15 P.M. (Letter from Anne P. Marsh, July 27, 1986)

(**#284**) July 27, 1986: Several people; Bulwagga Beach, Port Henry, NY; "a tail and some humps"; animal 120 ft. from shore; sighting at 7:30 P.M. (*Times of Ti*, August 12, 1986)

(**#285**) August 3, 1986: Brenda Baker and several others; Port Henry Beach Dock, Port Henry, NY; ". . . a long, black, snake-like thing rose to the surface of the water," said Baker; animal appeared near a water-skier floating on the water awaiting the tow boat's return; animal 25–30 ft. long and 1½ ft. high; range 100 ft. (Letter from Brenda Baker, August 22, 1986)

(**#286**) August 31, 1986; David Christensen; while boating with uncle and father between Willsboro Point, NY and Four Brothers Islands; "it looked like a snake standing on the water"; 5 ft. long neck and greyish-black in color; sighting at 5:30 P.M. (Letter from David Christensen, September 1, 1986)

(**#287**) April 25, 1987: Lennie French; Barber Point, near Westport, NY; 2 humps about 1½–2 ft. high with each hump separated by 2 ft. of water; greyish green-brown in color; lake mirror-calm; sighting at 3 P.M. (Letter from Richard Smith, July 24, 1987)

(**#288**) June 17, 1987: Dwight Burnham and wife; near Champlain Bridge, VT side; pair observed 10–15 ft. long object on lake; observed through field glasses; sighting at 6:15 A.M. (*Champlain Courier*, July 10, 1987)

(**#289**) June 23, 1987: Cedric E. Haskins; Keeler's Bay, South Hero, VT; head/neck seen; "between black and very dark brown" in color; head was "angular and sharp-snouted"; "very calm, bay was like glass"; range 200 ft.; sighting at 5 P.M. (Letter from Cedric E. Haskins, July 13, 1987 and completed sighting sheet, July 13, 1987)

(**#290**) July 4, 1987: Kathy Allmon Goodrich and husband; Basin Harbor, VT; while canoeing the pair saw animal with 2 distinct humps and a third hump just breaking water; animal dark in color; range 40–50 ft.; sighting lasted 30–40 sec. (Letter from Kathy Allmon Goodrich, July 13, 1987)

(**#291**) July 26, 1987: Alison, James, Lauren, and Nicky Murphy, and Richard Cowperthwait; south of Kimball Dock, VT; "a dark, sinuous object about 18 feet in length moving through the water," wrote Lauren Murphy; 3–4 humps (Alison and James Murphy claim they saw a head, described as being flat and dark); used binoculars during sighting; calm lake surface and clear; range ½ mi.; sighting at 8 P.M. (Sighting sheet from Lauren Murphy, August 31, 1987 and sighting sheet from Alison Murphy, September 3, 1987)

(**#292**) September 12, 1987: Marilynne and Brent Holden; Treadwell Bay, NY; saw "a young specimen of species"; "no distinguishabale head"; black, dull (not shiny) in color; only 3 ft. of animal visible; 2 humps observed; several photographs taken by Marilynne Holden using a Canon AE1 camera with 85–205 mm lens; lake surface almost calm with some chop; range 24 ft.; sighting at 4 P.M. (Letter and completed sighting sheet from Marilynne Holden, September 13, 1987)

(#293) September 13, 1987: Marilynne and Brent Holden and Irene and Bob Sinclair; Treadwell Bay, NY; they believed they saw same animal as September 12, 1987 sighting; they proposed the animal may have been feeding in shallows off their dock; sighting at 4–4:15 P.M. (Letter and completed sighting sheet from Marilynne Holden, September 13, 1987)

(#294) Circa 1979: Eric Mills; Long Point, VT; Champ's head as large as a basketball; fin or crest on back; estimated size of Champ was 20 ft. (Letter from Dorothy Mills, August 6, 1984)

(#295) Years ago: Norman Rabidoux; off Grand Isle, VT; "I saw all the birds, hundreds of birds, coming together and circling above the water," said Rabidoux. "And then Champ popped up . . ." (*Burlington Free Press*, October 19, 1987)

1984–1987 Champ-related Field Work Update

This section acts to update readers on Champ field investigations since the first edition of CHAMP—BEYOND THE LEGEND was published in 1984. This documents field expeditions undertaken by two groups: Wind & Whalebone Media Productions and the Lake Champlain Phenomena Investigation. For more details on their field work consult the publication: CRYPTOZOOLOGY—INTERDISCIPLINARY JOURNAL OF THE INTERNATIONAL SOCIETY OF CRYPTOZOOLOGY, issues 1984–1987.

1984

In August, 1984, Richard Smith's Wind & Whalebone Media Productions began their first field sessions at Lake Champlain in pursuit of the Champ phenomenon. Smith's team did 14 days of on site work, with four days of that as field tests. Based at Essex, New York, the intent of the group was to test an underwater video system deploying the camera in vertical, horizontal, and trawling modes. During the trawling modes, dead eels were trailed behind the camera as bait for a hungry Champ. A hydrophone donated by Ike Blonder was also utilized. Smith carried a 35 mm camera with 300 mm lens for surface surveillance.

Wind & Whalebone Media Productions reported no underwater, surface, or hydrophone contacts with Champ. Nevertheless, Smith was pleased with this initial test of his underwater video system and with the hydrophone efforts.

Wind & Whalebone Media Productions' work was coordinated by Richard Smith with the following people assisting: Wendy Lathrop, Dennis and Janet Hall, Lois and Ike Blonder, Fred Keller, A. Burger, Joseph W. Zarzynski, Paul Crane, Deanna Parsons, Joan Crane, John Durant, Ed Parsons, Chris Stokes, Jane Garland, Robert Durant, Margaret Light, Mae W. Smith, and David Olsen.

The L.C.P.I. field work in 1984 was 17 days long. Based primarily at Kimball Dock, Vermont, most work was done by M.P. Meaney and Joseph W. Zarzynski. Rod Canham, Ted Straiton, and Richard Smith assisted during some of that time.

Field work emphasis was on surface surveillance using an array of cameras, a Venus Scientific Night Sight (donated by Susan Schmidt), and a 13 foot long Avon inflatable boat for surface surveillance. Two scuba dives for reconnaissance purposes were conducted by Meaney, Canham, and Zarzynski. There were no Champ sightings made by the L.C.P.I. team.

Two different groups conducted side-scan sonar surveys at the lake in 1984. One team was led by Jim Kennard, a L.C.P.I. member, with Scott Hill, also a L.C.P.I. member, assisting. The other side-scan sonar expedition was fielded by the Champlain Maritime Society with John Fish as side-scan sonar technician and Arthur Cohn as project leader. Both these surveys were shipwreck search oriented. Neither team reported any sonar anomalies which might emanate from a Champ animal.

1985

During 1985, Wind & Whalebone Media Productions visited Lake Champlain to continue further Champ-related field work. Based at Essex, New York, Richard Smith and his colleagues spent 24 days on site and did 12 days of lake operations.

Using boats under 14 feet as work vessels Smith's group spent most of the time doing sounding work using an Apelco/Raytheon 201-C recording sonar. The team did report three mid-water sonar readings. "Although none may be said at this time to represent contacts with large, unknown animals," wrote Smith, "they merit further investigation . . ." Some hydrophoning work was done, too.

Assisting Smith: Wendy Lathrop, Ike and Lois Blonder, Gary Mangiacopra, John Andrews, Bob and Barbara Beach, the John Durant family, Dennis Hall, Joseph W. Zarzynski, Phil Keller, Ed Parsons, Robert Durant, Margaret Light, Peg McGeoch, and Jane Temple.

In 1985, the L.C.P.I. spent 31 days doing Champ-related field work at Lake Champlain. Work was done primarily by Meaney and Zarzynski with assistance from: Ted Straiton, Jack Sullivan, Bruce Hallenbeck, Ray and Salome Keller, Richard Smith, Ken Bartowski, Richard Cowperthwait, Lauren Murphy, John Becker, and Tim Clark. The work was done mostly from Kimball Dock, Vermont.

The L.C.P.I. did: day and night surface surveillance with 35 mm cameras, movie and television cameras, and a night sight; sonar work using a Raytheon DE725C sonar attached to a 4.5 foot tall aluminum tripod; scuba searches/scuba diver photography; and a search for a reported "skeleton remains of a whale" in the lake. Five scuba dives were made.

No Champ sightings or sonar contacts were recorded. However, the highlight of the L.C.P.I.'s 1985 field work may have been its search for a large skeleton of an animal in the lake. That underwater search was launched after archivists at the New York State Archives uncovered written references dating from 1919–1921 that remains of a whale-sized animal, possibly a Champ, were on the lake bottom. The subsurface search did not discover any physical evidence to support that, but further archival and field work into that reference may one day reveal more information on this remarkable story.

1986

In July, 1986, Wind & Whalebone Media Productions based at Essex, New York, conducted 21 days of research and field work at Lake Champlain. Assisting in operations and logistics: Phil Keller, Kip Cooper, Phil Houston, Wendy Lathrop, David Olsen, Ike and Lois Blonder, Tom Walko, Gil Fell, Joseph W. Zarzynski, Robert Durant, Margaret Light, Gary Mangiacopra, and Bill James.

The team conducted underwater video camera work and sonar surveying. The primary sonar was a Vexilar K-1200 chart recorder unit, with an Apelco/Raytheon 201C chart recorder also deployed. No photographic, video, or sonar recordings of Champ were made.

The L.C.P.I. team conducted 31 days of field investigations at the 109 mile long Lake Champlain in 1986. The L.C.P.I. worked mainly from Kimball Dock, Vermont. Most field work was again done by Meaney and Zarzynski with assistance from: Ted Straiton, Scott Hill, Jim Kennard, Marian Zarzynski, Liz Meaney, Don Mayland, Ken Bartowski, Richard Smith, and John Becker.

The L.C.P.I. work relied primarily upon surface surveillance using cameras, binoculars, and a night sight. Boat deployed sonar (Raytheon DE725C) was done from a 13 foot Avon inflatable. Five Champ-related scuba dives were made with divers using an underwater still camera and underwater video camera. No photographic, video, or sonar recordings of Champ were made by any L.C.P.I. personnel.

1987

In July, 1987, Richard Smith and William L. Konrad teamed up at Lake Champlain (Essex, New York) to conduct sonar work in search of the Champ animals. Smith, Konrad, and associates were at the lake for 14 days with six of those days spent sonar searching. The principal sonar used was a 112 kHz unit with a line scan OSR-219 recorder. Much of this system was designed by Konrad and Olsen. The function of this unit was to "extend a sonar beam horizontally across the lake's central basin" to monitor for Champ. They also hoped to "make additional vertical sonar chart recordings of the lake basin from a boat." Due to restrictive water conditions the team's primary sonar system could only record at a distance of 1,250 feet, and not the gear's 3 mile potential. A secondary sonar unit (Apelco/Raytheon 201-C chart recorder) was also deployed. Surface surveillance with cameras/binoculars was conducted, too.

No recordings or sightings of Champ were made though valuable experience testing these sonar units was gained in 1987 by Smith and Konrad. Assisting Smith and Konrad in 1987 were: Ike and Lois Blonder, Gary Mangiacopra, Phil Keller, Werner Larsen, Wendy Lathrop, Margaret Light, Morris and Ellin Glenn, Katherine Teetor, Joseph W. Zarzynski, Robert Durant, David Olsen, and Arthur Cohn.

John Becker working with the L.C.P.I. during 1987 field work at Lake Champlain. Becker is testing a video digitizer monitoring system which will be used in future expeditions to observe the lake's surface and underwater to activate a video recorder when unusual movement — possibly from a Champ — is detected. (photo credit: Joseph W. Zarzynski)

1987 marked a new era in underwater exploration technology for the L.C.P.I. in its Champ search. The more conventional forms of "monster hunting" like surface surveillance with cameras from shore and boat, scuba searches, and night scope use were again done. However, 1987 saw more sophisticated equipment such as side-scan sonar, a ROV (remotely-operated-vehicle), and a video digitizer monitoring system employed.

The L.C.P.I. conducted 30 days of field work in 1987 exploring for the Lake Champlain mystery animals. Most of that time was spent doing conventional lake monster searching. However, six days of that time were devoted to "Project 'Champ' Carcass," a systematic search of a small part of Lake Champlain to try to locate a carcass of a Champ animal. That unique search, what is probably the first of its kind to deploy a side-scan sonar to search for carcass-sized targets and then to eyeball them using an underwater robot called a ROV, was made possible when firms donated sophisticated search gear to the L.C.P.I. Kaselaan & D'Angelo

This Klein side-scan sonar record (500 kHz) was made on August 7, 1987 during "Project 'Champ' Carcass." The record is of a shipwreck, probably the tugboat WILLIAM H. MCALLISTER. That vessel sank in November, 1963 and it lies in approximately 150 feet of water. The shipwreck sonar discovery is a by-product result of monster searching. (courtesy: Klein Associates, Inc. and L.C.P.I.)

Associates, Inc., Haddon Heights, New Jersey, and Klein Associates, Inc., Salem, New Hampshire, donated a MiniRover Mk II ROV and a Klein 500 kHz and 100 kHz side-scan sonar. Vermont Dive Charter assisted with reduced rates on renting its 28 foot long *NEPTUNE STAR* vessel.

Two 3-day search sessions were conducted — June 26–28 and August 7–9. Participating in "Project 'Champ' Carcass" were: Chip D'Angelo, Vince Capone, Garry Kozak, M.P. Meaney, Joseph W. Zarzynski, Dr. Russ Bellico, Don Mayland, Captain Rafael Veve, Captain Dan Couture, Jim Rock, Patxi Pastor, and Willie Veve. Areas searched were: off Burlington, Vermont; off Colchester Reef, Vermont; Malletts Bay, Vermont; with most of the effort near Schuyler Island, New York. The majority of surveying off Schuyler Island was a side-scan sonar search using a Loran navigational system for precise vessel runs. The side-scan sonar operator was Garry Kozak, Manager — Field Operations, Klein Associates, Inc., with Vince Capone, Division Manager — Marine & Aquatic Sciences, Kaselaan & D'Angelo Associates, Inc., as the ROV pilot. Marty Klein of Klein Associates, Inc. and Chip

Chip D'Angelo (in scuba suit), President of Kaselaan & D'Angelo Associates, Inc., and the author, Joseph W. Zarzynski, with an underwater robot called ROV (remotely operated vehicle). Kaselaan & D'Angelo Associates, Inc. donated the ROV to the L.C.P.I. for Champ-related field operations. (photo credit: M.P. Meaney)

D'Angelo of Kaselaan & D'Angelo Associates, Inc. greatly assisted the L.C.P.I. by the donation of gear from their companies.

Several interesting sonar targets were noted that will be ROV inspected in 1988. The most productive sonar discovery was not Champ-related, but came on August 7, when the Klein 500 kHz unit recorded a shipwreck. The wreck, lying in about 150 feet of water, is most likely a tugboat and is probably the 86 foot long *WILLIAM H. MCALLISTER*. Built during World War II as the ST-243 it was later renamed *WILLIAM H. MCALLISTER*. It sank on November 17, 1963 after hitting Schuyler Reef. Fortunately all crew members survived. During the Summer, 1988 a team from Kaselaan & D'Angelo Associates, Inc. intends to use their ROV, equipped with video and 35 mm cameras, to survey this wreck, a fascinating find made during a lake monster hunt. Oral history indicates the vessel was probably dived upon by a salvage scuba team shortly after the mishap, but information on that is vague. The sonar discovery of the vessel has been reported to the Office of the State Archeologist – New York State. Anyone with more knowledge about the *WILLIAM H. MCALLISTER* is asked to contact Joseph W. Zarzynski, P.O. Box 2134, Wilton, New York 12866, USA.

Since "Project 'Champ' Carcass" had access to a ROV equipped with a manipulator arm which could retrieve small objects, it was decided that if a Champ carcass was discovered in deep waters, that a skin sample should be secured for scientific study. Dr. George Zug of the National Museum of Natural History at the Smithsonian Institution, Washington, D.C. was kind enough to advise on procedures to preserve tissue samples for transfer to members of the scientific community. Vince Capone, "Project 'Champ' Carcass" ROV pilot and project science officer, did bring along the necessary storage facilities to preserve a sample of Champ should a carcass have been found. The L.C.P.I. does not advocate killing a Champ to secure such a carcass, rather we believe that if these animals live, then they must die, and thus a bottom search of the lake may prove scientifically rewarding. By securing such a carcass, a major step would be taken leading to Champ's formal recognition, which would ensure protection for the species.

The experimentation of the use of a video digitizer monitoring system was another factor in making the L.C.P.I.'s 1987 field work its most sophisticated to date. John Becker was the coordinator of that project. The idea of this system was to use a surveillance camera to monitor the lake and to turn on a video recorder when movement was detected. By using a computer, camera, digitizer, and appropriate computer software this was feasible. These experiments were based at Kimball Dock, Vermont, from August 1–4, 1987. Such a system can record lake surface movement from boats, surface wakes, and possibly even – a Champ animal.

Assisting the L.C.P.I. during 1987 in surface surveillance for Champ: Ted Straiton, Bruce Hallenbeck, Jack Sullivan, David Pitkin, Ken Bartowski, and Karen Lichter. Valuable input was provided by Richard Smith of Wind & Whalebone Media Productions.

The Future

Wind & Whalebone Media Productions and the L.C.P.I. plan to continue field work at Lake Champlain meeting the challenge to identify the Champ colony. I hope this new edition of CHAMP – BEYOND THE LEGEND provides a record of the story of Champ and acts to encourage more individuals and groups to work toward conquering this zoological Mt. Everest.

If the recent Champ field work is an accurate barometer of things to come, it appears the near future holds exciting times and dramatic discoveries as more people and groups show a sincere and inquisitive interest in trying to solve the Champ jigsaw puzzle. As this incredible drama continues to unfold there is one main question that still after all these years continues to perplex, yet motivate me, "What lies beyond this legend called 'Champ'?"

Notes

1. Glenn E. Myer and Gerhard K. Gruendling, preparers, *Limnology of Lake Champlain* (Plattsburgh, January, 1979), p. 2.

2. *Ibid.*, pp. 12–19.

3. Richard Dworsky et al., *Lake Champlain Atlas: Water Quality and Shoreland Use* (Boston, August, 1978), pp. 5–8.

4. *Lake Champlain Planning Guide: For Water and Related Land Resources*, sponsored by State of New York, State of Vermont, and The New England River Basins Commission (June, 1976), pp. 61–63.

5. Joseph W. Zarzynski, "Champ—A Zoological Jigsaw Puzzle," *Adirondack Bits 'n Pieces*, Vol. 1, No. 1 (1983), p. 17.

6. Dr. Bernard Heuvelmans, "What Is Cryptozoology?", *Cryptozoology: Interdisciplinary Journal of the International Society of Cryptozoology*, translated Ron Westrum, Vol. 1 (Winter 1982), p. 1.

7. John Noble Wilford, "Society Formed to Bring Them Back, Alive," *New York Times*, January 19, 1982.

8. *The Living Coelacanth*, British Museum of Natural History, Leaflet No. 10 (1975).

9. Janet L. Hopson, "Fins to feet to Fanclubs: An (Old) Fish Story," *Science News*, Vol. 109, No. 2 (January 10, 1976), pp. 28–30.

10. *The Living Coelacanth.*

11. The International Society of Cryptozoology information sheet.

12. Ian Anderson, "Goodbye Jaws, hello Lips," *New Scientist*, (October 27, 1983), p. 266 and Walter Sullivan, "Bizarre Sharks Come to Light," *New York Times*, October 25, 1983.

13. Anderson.

14. Dr. Roy P. Mackal, *Searching for Hidden Animals* (Garden City, 1980), p. xiii.

15. *Ibid.*

16. J. Richard Greenwell, ed., *The ISC Newsletter*, Vol. 1, No. 1 (Spring 1982).

17. The International Society of Cryptozoology information sheet.

Notes

18. Nicholas Witchell, *Loch Ness and the Monster* (Inverness, 1975), p. 2.

19. *Ibid.*

20. Adrian Shine, "The biology of Loch Ness," *New Scientist*, (February 17, 1983).

21. Nicholas Witchell, *The Loch Ness Story* (Lavenham, 1974), p. 13.

22. Hill, p. 207 and Mackal, *The Monsters of Loch Ness*, p. 84 and William Owen, *Scotland's Loch Ness Monster* (Norwich, no copyright date) and Shine and Nicholas Witchell, *The Loch Ness Story* (London, 1982), p. 31.

23. George R. Hamell, Letter to Joseph W. Zarzynski, August 1, 1983.

24. Hill, pp. 15–16.

25. George R. Hamell, "Of Hockers, Diamonds and Hourglasses – Some Interpretations of Seneca Archeological Art," Paper presented at Iroquois Conference at Albany, New York, October 13–15, 1979.

26. Nigel Sitwell, "The Loch Ness Monster Evidence," *Wildlife* (March, 1976), p. 106.

27. Morris F. Glenn, *The Story of Three Towns: Westport, Essex, and Willsboro, New York* (Alexandria, 1977), p. 82.

28. Warwick Stevens Carpenter, *The Summer Paradise in History* (Albany, 1914), p. 113.

29. Nathan L. Swayze, *Engraved Powder Horns* (Yazoo City, 1978), p. 81.

30. Dr. Philip Reines, Letter to J. Robert DuBois, November 15, 1983.

31. Donald J. Orth, Letter to Joseph W. Zarzynski, April 14, 1978.

32. William S. Ellis, "Loch Ness—The Lake and the Legend," *National Geographic*, Vol. 151, No. 6 (June, 1977), pp. 759–779 and Witchell, *The Loch Ness Story*.

33. Edward F. Kehoe, Letter to Joseph W. Zarzynski, March 11, 1982.

34. Sandra Mansi, Completed sighting sheet sent to Joseph W. Zarzynski, January 14, 1980.

35. Randall Beach, "Family album contains picture of the 'Champ,'" *The New Haven Register*, November 14, 1981.

36. Dr. George Zug, Letter to Joseph W. Zarzynski, July 9, 1980.

37. "'Champ' photo real, experts conclude," *Albany Times-Union*, May 2, 1981.

38. Dr. B. Roy Frieden, "Interim Report/Lake Champlain 'Monster' Photograph," April 30, 1981.

39. Dr. Paul H. LeBlond, "An Estimate Of The Dimensions Of The Lake Champlain Monster From The Length Of Adjacent Wind Waves In The Mansi Photograph," *Cryptozoology: Interdisciplinary Journal of the International Society of Cryptozoology*, Vol. 1 (Winter 1982), pp. 54–61.

40. Richard D. Smith, Letter to Joseph W. Zarzynski, November 23, 1983.

41. Witchell, *The Loch Ness Story*, 1974, p. 115.

42. Mackal, *The Monsters of Loch Ness*, p. 131.

43. Howard S. Curtis, ed., *Academy of Applied Science — Report to the Membership*, 1982, p. 28.

44. Richard Zitrin, "Diving for Treasures in the Deep," *Rochester Times-Union*, January 17, 1980.

45. Raymond W. Sargent, Completed sighting sheet sent to Joseph W. Zarzynski, June 8, 1982.

46. Raymond W. Sargent, Letter to Joseph W. Zarzynski, July 5, 1982.

47. Clive Cussler, Letter to Joseph W. Zarzynski, August, 1981.

48. Shine.

49. Mackal, *Searching for Hidden Animals*, pp. 228–229.

50. *Ibid.*, p. 232.

51. A.H. Saxon, ed., *Selected Letters of P.T. Barnum* (New York, 1983), pp. 290-291.

52. *Whitehall Times*, November 5, 1873.

53. Leo O'Conner, "W. Douglas Burden Foresees a 'Natural' Fate for Mankind," *Burlington Free Press*, August 6, 1974.

54. Heuvelmans, p. 8.

55. Reines.

56. Robert G. Werner, *Freshwater Fishes of New York State — A Field Guide* (Syracuse, 1980), p. 51.

57. William T. Hornaday, *Hornaday's American Natural History* (New York, 1927), p. 427.

58. Daniel S. Plosila, Letter to Joseph W. Zarzynski, May 28, 1982.

59. Anthony G. Harmsworth, *The Mysterious Monsters of Loch Ness* (Drumnadrochit, 1980), p. 23.

60. "Prehistoric Reptiles Ate Rocks," GEO (July 1981).

61. *Albany Times-Union.*

62. Richard D. Smith, "Research Into Large Unidentified Animals Of Freshwater Lakes ('The Lake Monsters')," March, 1983, p. 3.

63. H.R. 19 Vermont House of Representatives, April 20, 1982.

64. Hal Bowser, "Vanished," *Science Digest*, Vol. 90, No. 7 (July 1980), p. 50.

65. Witchell, *The Loch Ness Story* (1974), p. 15.

66. Mackal, Letter to Joseph W. Zarzynski, December 2, 1983.

67. Dr. C.L. Smith, "What if there is no 'Champ'?", December 1, 1983, pp. 3-4.

68. *Ibid.*

Author's Note: The works cited in this bibliography include only those directly referred to in the writing of the book manuscript. This bibliography does not include sources used for the appendices or works referred to in the text of the book manuscript.

Bibliography

Anderson, Ian. "Goodbye Jaws, hello Lips," *New Scientist*. (October 27, 1983).

Beach, Randall. "Family album contains picture of the 'Champ,' " *The New Haven Register*. New Haven, Connecticut, November 14, 1981.

Biggar, H.P., ed. *The Works of Samuel de Champlain*. Toronto, Ontario, Canada, 1925, Vol. 2.

Bowser, Hal. "Vanished," *Science Digest*. Vol. 90, No. 7(July 1982).

Carpenter, Warwick Stevens. *The Summer Paradise in History*. Albany, New York, 1914.

Carroll, Robert W., Jr. Letter to J. Robert DuBois, March 7, 1984.

Carroll, Robert W., Jr. Letter to Joseph W. Zarzynski, April 2, 1984.

Carruth, Father J.A. *Loch Ness and Its Monster*. Fort Augustus, Scotland, 1971.

Casale, Assemblyman Anthony J. Letter to Joseph W. Zarzynski, April 26, 1983.

" 'Champ' photo real, experts conclude," *Albany Times-Union*. Albany, New York, May 2, 1981.

Church, Tim. "Flathead Lake Monster: A Preliminary Report." March

21, 1975.

Countryman, William D. "Checklist of the Recent Fishes of Vermont." Vermont Department of Fish and Game, Agency of Environmental Conservation, October, 1975.

Curtis, Howard S., ed. *Academy of Applied Science — Report to the Membership.* 1982.

Cussler, Clive. Letter to Joseph W. Zarzynski, August, 1981.

Dinsdale, Tim. *Monster Hunt.* Washington, D.C., 1972.

Dworsky, Richard et al. *Lake Champlain Atlas: Water Quality and Shoreland Use.* Boston, Massachusetts, August, 1978.

Ellis, William S. "Loch Ness — The Lake and the Legend," *National Geographic.* Vol. 151, No. 6(June 1977).

Frieden, Dr. B. Roy. "Interim Report/Lake Champlain 'Monster' Photograph." April 30, 1981.

Glenn, Morris F. *The Story of Three Towns: Westport, Essex, and Willsboro, New York.* Alexandria, Virginia, 1977.

Greenwell, J. Richard, ed. *The ISC Newsletter.* Vol. 1, No. 1(Spring 1982).

_____. *The ISC Newsletter.* Vol. 2, No. 1(Spring 1983).

Hamell, George R. Letter to Joseph W. Zarzynski, August 1, 1983.

_____. "Of Hockers, Diamonds and Hourglasses — Some Interpretations of Seneca Archeological Art." Paper presented at Iroquois Conference at Albany, New York, October 13–15, 1979.

Harmsworth, Anthony G. *The Mysterious Monsters of Loch Ness.* Drumnadrochit, Scotland, 1980.

Heuvelmans, Dr. Bernard. Letter to Joseph W. Zarzynski, January 29, 1983.

_____. "What Is Cryptozoology?", *Cryptozoology: Interdisciplinary Journal of the International Society of Cryptozoology.* Translated by Ron Westrum, Vol. 1(Winter 1982).

Hill, Ralph Nading. *Lake Champlain: Key to Liberty.* Montpelier, Vermont, 1977.

Hornaday, William T. *Hornaday's American Natural History.* New York, New York, 1927.

Hopson, Janet L. "Fins to feet to Fanclubs:An (Old) Fish Story," *Science News.* Vol. 109, No. 2(January 10, 1976).

The International Society of Cryptozoology information sheet.

James, Paul N., ed. *The Klein Line.* No. 2(May 1982).

_____. *The Klein Line.* No. 4(June 1983).

Bibliography

Johnson, Charles W. *The Nature of Vermont.* Hanover, New Hampshire, 1980.

Kehoe, Edward F. Letter to Joseph W. Zarzynski, March 11, 1982.

Klein, Marty. Letter to Joseph W. Zarzynski, November 3, 1982.

Lake Champlain Planning Guide: For Water and Related Land Resources. Sponsored by State of New York, State of Vermont, and the New England River Basins Commission, June, 1976.

LeBlond, Dr. Paul H. "An Estimate Of The Dimensions Of The Lake Champlain Monster From The Length Of Adjacent Wind Waves In The Mansi Photograph," *Cryptozoology: Interdisciplinary Journal of the International Society of Cryptozoology.* Vol. 1(Winter 1982).

The Living Coelacanth. British Museum of Natural History, Leaflet No. 10(1975).

Mackal, Dr. Roy P. Letter to Joseph W. Zarzynski, December 2, 1983.

_____. *The Monsters of Loch Ness.* Chicago, Illinois, 1976.

_____. *Searching For Hidden Animals.* Garden City, New York, 1980.

Mangiacopra, Gary S. "Lake Champlain: America's Loc Ness – Part Two," *Of Sea and Shore.* (Summer 1978).

Mansi, Sandra. Completed sighting sheet sent to Joseph W. Zarzynski, January 14, 1980.

Moon, Mary. *Ogopogo.* Vancouver, British Columbia, Canada, 1977.

Morse, Thomas E. Completed sighting sheet sent to Joseph W. Zarzynski, October 8, 1980.

Myer, Glenn E. and Gerhard K. Greundling, preparers. *Limnology of Lake Champlain.* Plattsburgh, New York, January, 1979.

O'Conner, Leo. "W. Douglas Burden Foresees a 'Natural' Fate for Mankind," *Burlington Free Press,* Burlington, Vermont, August 6, 1974.

Orth, Donald J. Letter to Joseph W. Zarzynski, April 14, 1978.

Owen, William. *Scotland's Loch Ness Monster.* Norwich, United Kingdom, no copyright date.

Plosila, Daniel S. Letter to Joseph W. Zarzynski, May 28, 1982.

"Prehistoric Reptiles Ate Rocks," *Geo.* (July 1981).

Reines, Dr. Philip. Letter to J. Robert DuBois, November 15, 1983.

Resolution – Adopted By The Village of Port Henry Trustees. On October 6, 1980.

Rhodes, Dean. "Expert links monster sightings," *Bangor Daily News.* Bangor, Maine, December 30, 1977.

Sargent, Raymond W. Completed sighting sheet sent to Joseph W. Zarzynski, June 8, 1982.

Sargent, Raymond W. Letter to Joseph W. Zarzynski, July 5, 1982.

Saxon, A.H., ed. *Selected Letters of P.T. Barnum.* New York, New York, 1983.

Senate Calendar. Montpelier, Vermont, February 26, 1981.

Shine, Adrian. "The biology of Loch Ness," *New Scientist.* February 17, 1983.

Sitwell, Nigel. "The Loch Ness Monster Evidence," *Wildlife.* (March 1976).

Smith, Dr. C.L. "What if there is no 'Champ'?" December 1, 1983.

Smith, Richard D. Letter to Joseph W. Zarzynski, November 23, 1983.

_____. "Research Into Large Unidentified Animals Of Freshwater Lakes ('The Lake Monsters')". March, 1983.

Sullivan, Walter. "Bizarre Sharks Come To Light," *New York Times.* New York, New York, October 25, 1983.

Swayze, Nathan L. *Engraved Powder Horns.* Yazoo City, Mississippi, 1978.

Tucker, Louis L. Letter to Mayor Erastus Corning, December 24, 1975.

Vermont Fish & Game Digest of Fish & Game Laws. 1982.

Werner, Robert G. *Freshwater Fishes of New York State—A Field Guide.* Syracuse, New York, 1980.

Whitehall Times. November 5, 1873.

Whyte, Constance. *More Than a Legend.* London, United Kingdom, 1957.

Wilford, John Noble. "Society Formed to Bring Them Back, Alive," *New York Times.* New York, New York, January 19, 1982.

Witchell, Nicholas. *Loch Ness and the Monster.* Inverness, Scotland, 1975.

_____. *The Loch Ness Story.* Lavenham, Suffolk, United Kingdom, 1974.

_____. London, United Kingdom, 1982.

"Wrecked ship found off L.I., author says," *The Evening Press.* Binghamton, New York, October 12, 1983.

Zarzynski, Joseph W. "Champ—A Zoological Jigsaw Puzzle," *Adirondack Bits 'n Pieces.* Vol. 1, No. 1(1983).

_____. ed., *Champ Channels.* Vol. 1, No. 2(August 1983).

Zitrin, Richard. "Diving for Treasures in the Deep," *Rochester Times-Union.* Rochester, New York, January 17, 1980.

Zug, Dr. George. Letter to Joseph W. Zarzynski, July 9, 1980.

Index

JOSEPH W. ZARZYNSKI has been investigating lake phenomena since 1974. His special interest is in the Champ animals of Lake Champlain, and he has travelled to Scotland's Loch Ness eight times on research projects. He is a member of numerous scientific and research organizations including: the International Society of Cryptozoology, the Atlantic Alliance for Maritime Heritage Conservation, the Atlantic Alliance Lake George Bateaux Research Team, Champlain Maritime Society, the Loch Ness Wellington Association, Ltd., the Loch Ness and Morar Project, the Society for the Investigation of the Unexplained, and the International Fortean Organization. Zarzynski is a "Fellow" in The Explorers Club and is an honorary member of the Loch Ness Association of Explorers.

Mr. Zarzynski requests that any new Champ sighting information be submitted to him at the following address:

LAKE CHAMPLAIN PHENOMENA INVESTIGATION
P.O. Box 2134
WILTON, NEW YORK 12866 USA